SCHOLASTIC

Cut & Paste Mini-Books
Around the Year

NANCY I. SANDERS

New York • Toronto • London • Auckland • Sydney
Mexico City • New Delhi • Hong Kong • Buenos Aires

Teaching *Resources*

To Mrs. Betty Bryant, from Everett Area Elementary School, who was my fifth grade teacher. Your gentle manners, kind wisdom, and astute guidance taught me many things beyond the required book knowledge you diligently presented to blossoming minds. Seeing you read your Bible during lunch still inspires me today!

To Mrs. Mary Lee Quinn, from Everett Area High School, who went beyond the required role of a teacher and taught me Spanish III one-on-one during the summer months. Your sweet example and friendship opened a treasury of knowledge I still value today. Thanks for fostering a love for the importance of education!

Scholastic Inc. grants teachers permission to photocopy the reproducible pages in this book for classroom use. No other part of this publication may be reproduced in whole or in part, or stored in a retrieval system, or transmitted in any form or by any means, electronic, photocopying, recording, or otherwise, without written permission of the publisher. For information regarding permission, write to Scholastic Inc., 557 Broadway, New York, NY 10012-3999.

Edited by Immacula A. Rhodes
Cover design by Jason Robinson
Interior illustrations by Lucia Kemp Henry
Interior design by Holly Grundon

ISBN: 978-0-439-60631-8

Copyright © 2011 by Nancy I. Sanders
Illustrations © 2011 by Scholastic Inc.
Published by Scholastic Inc.
All rights reserved.
Printed in the U.S.A.

1 2 3 4 5 6 7 8 9 10   40   18 17 16 15 14 13 12 11

Contents

Mini-Book	Skill	Page

Introduction

Welcome to *Cut & Paste Mini-Books: Around the Year*! These 15 mini-books raise the use of manipulatives to a fun and educational level. Designed to enhance your curriculum, the stories reinforce important standards-based concepts and literacy skills as children read the text and glue patterns onto the corresponding pages to demonstrate comprehension.

In the mini-books, you'll find a collection of stories about holidays, special days, and seasons that occur around the year. The use of high-frequency words and controlled vocabulary makes the mini-books just right for helping beginning readers build word recognition, fluency, and other literacy skills. Built-in concepts align with the Mid-continent Research for Education and Learning (McREL) standards for Kindergarten and first grade, giving children practice in essential skills across the curriculum, such as using context clues, recognizing number and color words, making inferences, counting, comparing sizes, identifying shapes, using the five senses, and understanding sun safety. Each story prompts children to think about a specific topic related to that particular time of the year and then respond by gluing patterns onto the pages to complete the book.

Everything you need to make the mini-books is here. As children follow the directions to assemble the books, they'll get additional practice in sequencing and building fine motor skills. Each reproducible mini-book includes patterns that children cut out and paste onto the pages. Suggestions for introducing the topic are provided to help you prepare children to complete the mini-book successfully. The extension activities let you elaborate on the topic or take the skill a step further to help reinforce it.

Children will love revisiting these stories again and again. As they read, they'll enjoy practicing important skills in a fun, unique way. In addition, children will gain confidence in word recognition and reading fluency with repeated readings. But don't keep all the fun at school—encourage children to take the mini-books home, where they can continue and share their learning excitement with their families!

Using the Mini-Books

Once children have assembled their mini-books, you might walk them through the pages as a preview before they glue the pieces in place. Here are some suggestions for doing this:

- Ask children to place all of the patterns face-up near their mini-book.
- Beginning with the cover, read aloud the text on each page.
- If a page has a blank for children to fill in, talk about what they need to do to find the answer to write in that blank, but tell them not to fill it in yet.

* As you preview each right-hand page, encourage children to use clues from the text on the spread to decide which pattern belongs on the page. Invite them to place the pattern on the page (but not glue it down yet) and then read the text again. Does the pattern make sense with the text? When finished, ask them to put the pattern back with the others.

* When you preview page 11 of the mini-book (the last page), talk about what children need to do to complete the activity. If desired, work together to find the answers, but have children wait until later to fill in the answers.

* After previewing the mini-book together, have children read it by themselves. This time, ask them to fill in the blanks, glue each pattern to its corresponding page, and complete the activity on page 11.

Assembling the Mini-Books

The cut-and-paste mini-books require very few materials, and children can complete them at their desk or a learning center. To get started, provide children with copies of the reproducible pages for the selected mini-book, then demonstrate the steps below. (Or you might assemble the books in advance.)

Materials

* scissors

* crayons or markers

* glue stick or paste

* stapler

1. Fold the front cover/page 1 in half along the solid center line. Keep the fold to the right side.

2. Repeat step 1 for each of the remaining page pairs: pages 2/3, 4/5, 6/7, 8/9, and 10/11. Stack the pages in order with the cover on top and all of the folds on the right side.

3. Staple the pages together along the left edge.

Connections to the Standards

Connections to the McREL Standards

Mid-continent Research for Education and Learning (McREL), a nationally recognized nonprofit organization, has compiled and evaluated national and state standards—and proposed what teachers should provide for their K–1 students to grow proficient in reading and other content areas. The activities in this book support the following standards:

Reading
* Uses mental images based on pictures and print to aid in comprehension of text
* Predicts story events or outcomes, using illustrations and prior knowledge as a guide
* Uses basic elements of phonetic and structural analysis to decode unknown words
* Understands level-appropriate sight words and vocabulary
* Uses self-correction strategies

Math
* Counts whole numbers
* Understands symbolic, concrete, and pictorial representations of numbers
* Understands strategies for the addition and subtraction of whole numbers
* Knows basic geometric language for naming shapes
* Understands basic properties of simple geometric shapes
* Sorts and groups objects by attributes

Science
* Knows that plants and animals closely resemble their parents
* Knows that living things go through a process of growth and change
* Knows vocabulary for different kinds of weather (e.g., *rainy*, *windy*, *sunny*)
* Knows how the environment changes over the seasons

Behavioral Studies
* Knows that people use their senses to find out about their surroundings and themselves and that different senses provide different information

Health
* Knows basic personal hygiene habits required to maintain health

History
* Understands the contributions and significance of historical figures
* Understands how individuals have worked to achieve the liberties and equality promised in the principles of American democracy and to improve the lives of people from many groups
* Understands the daily life of a colonial community
* Understands the reasons that Americans celebrate certain national holidays
* Understands personal family or cultural heritage through stories, songs, and celebrations
* Knows why important buildings, statues, and monuments (e.g., the White House) are associated with national history

Kendall, J. S., & Marzano, R. J. (2004). *Content knowledge: A compendium of standards and benchmarks for K-12 education.* Aurora, CO: Mid-continent Research for Education and Learning. Online database: http://www.mcrel.org/standards-benchmarks/

Ready for School!

Skill   Context Clues

Getting Started

Ask children to tell about the things they do to get ready for school. Write their responses on chart paper. Then give each child a sheet of white construction paper that has been folded in half twice to create four sections. Have children illustrate and label each section with an activity they do to prepare for school. Encourage them to use drawings that correspond to their text. As children share their pictures with the class, talk about how the illustrations and text support each other.

Completing the Mini-Book

Ask children to write their name on the cover, then cut out and glue the patterns onto the pages, as shown. Finally, have them complete the activity on the last page.

Reproducible Pages
mini-book:
pages 8–13
patterns: page 14

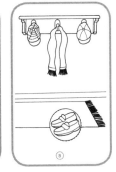

Draw an X on the item that does not belong in each row.

Taking It Further

Brainstorm a list of things children might do at night to prepare for the next school day, such as complete their homework, pack school supplies in their bookbag, and set out the clothes they'll wear. Then have each child write a different activity from the list on each of five index cards and illustrate that activity on the back. Punch a hole in the top left corner of each child's cards, bind them with a metal ring, and have the child use the cards as a nightly reminder to prepare ahead for the next school day.

Here's my lunch to put in a sack.

Ready for School!

SCHOOL BUS

by _____

Here are books to put in my pack.

Cut & Paste Mini-Books: Around the Year © 2011 by Nancy I. Sanders, Scholastic Teaching Resources (page 9)

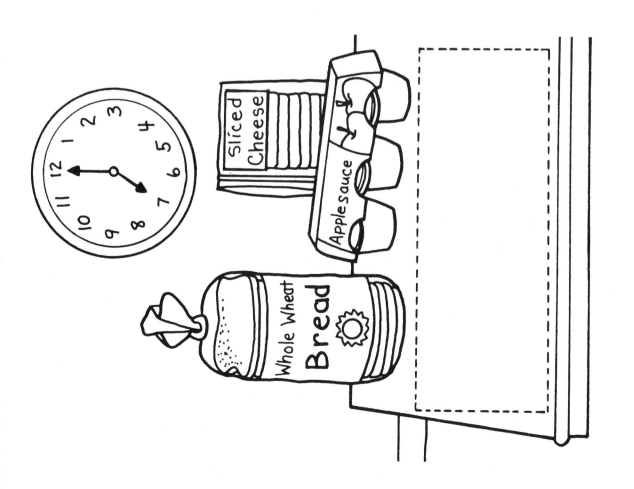

Here's an apple for my teacher's treat.

Cut & Paste Mini-Books: Around the Year © 2011 by Nancy I. Sanders, Scholastic Teaching Resources (page 10)

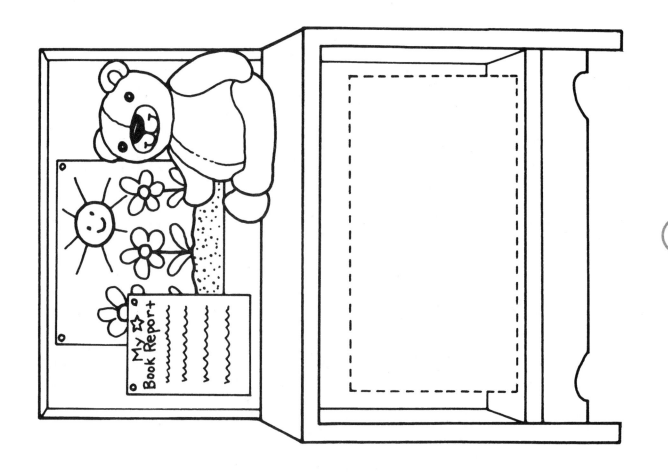

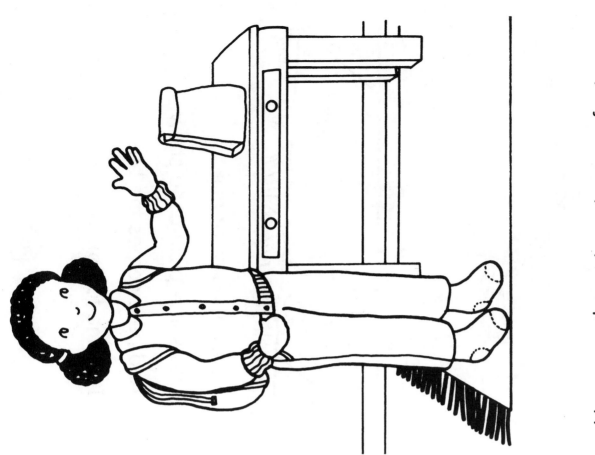

Here are shoes to put on my feet.

Cut & Paste Mini-Books: Around the Year © 2011 by Nancy I. Sanders, Scholastic Teaching Resources (page 11)

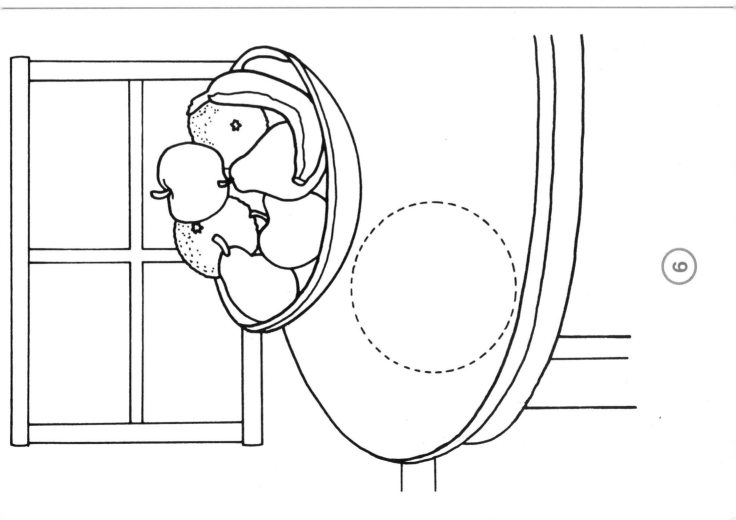

6

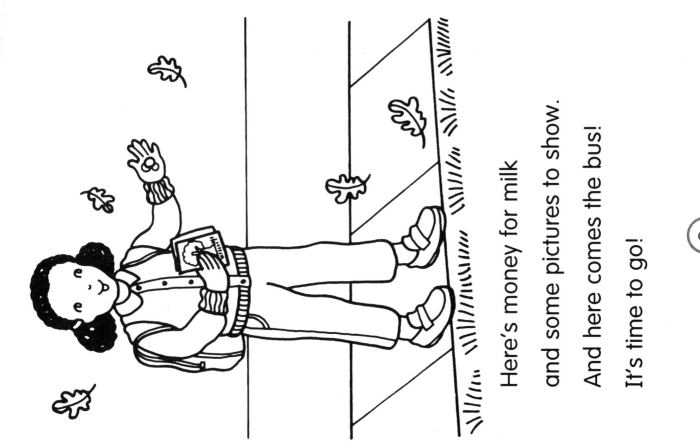

Here's money for milk
and some pictures to show.
And here comes the bus!
It's time to go!

⑨

Cut & Paste Mini-Books: Around the Year © 2011 by Nancy I. Sanders, Scholastic Teaching Resources (page 12)

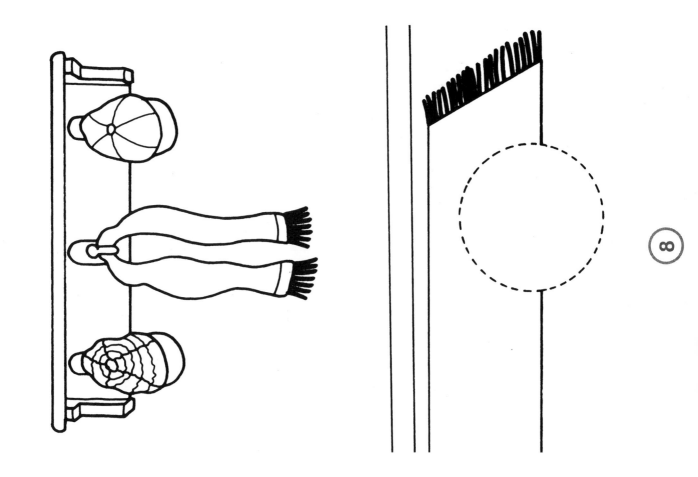

⑧

Look at each row. Which one does not belong? Put an X on it.

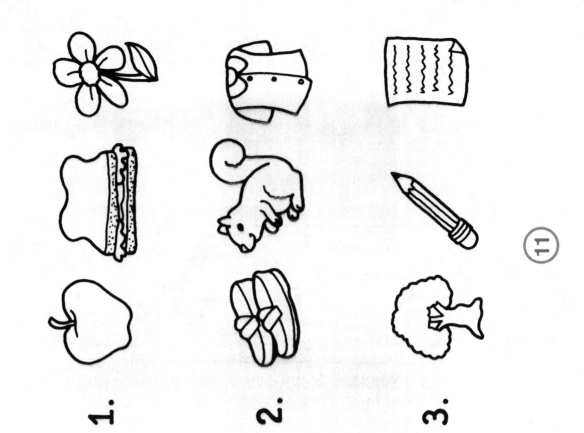

1.

2.

3.

Cut & Paste Mini-Books: Around the Year © 2011 by Nancy I. Sanders, Scholastic Teaching Resources (page 13)

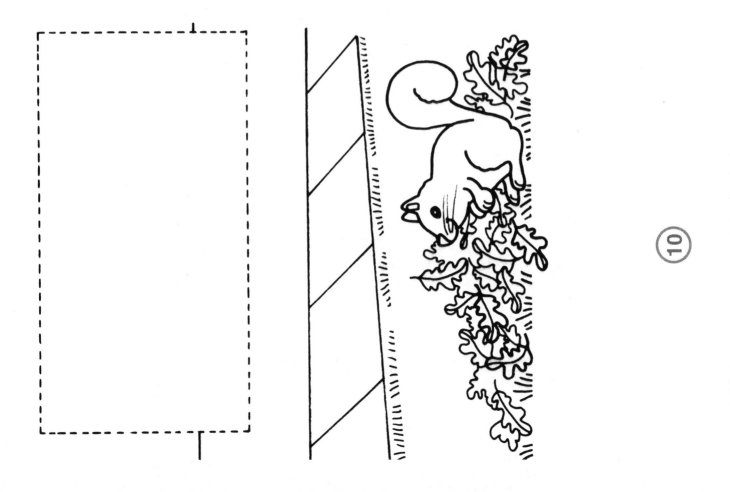

Ready for School!

Cut & Paste Patterns

Cut & Paste Mini-Books: Around the Year © 2011 by Nancy I. Sanders, Scholastic Teaching Resources

Apples in the Tree

Skill Simple Subtraction

Getting Started

Put ten paper apples in a basket. Take out one apple at a time, counting as you go, and place it on a large sheet of green construction paper cut to represent the shape of a treetop. Then invite children to solve simple subtraction problems using the apples. For instance, you might ask a child to "pick" two apples to put in the basket and then tell how many are left in the tree. Have children return the removed apples to the tree when their turn ends.

Completing the Mini-Book

Ask children to write their name on the cover, then cut out and glue the patterns onto the pages, as shown. Finally, have them complete the activity on the last page.

Reproducible Pages
mini-book: pages 16–21
patterns: page 22

Apples in the Tree

by _____

10 apples are in the tree.
A baker picks 3 to make a pie.
How many apples are left for me?

①

_____ apples are in the tree!

②

7 apples are in the tree.
A boy picks 1 to give his teacher.
How many apples are left for me?

③

_____ apples are in the tree!

④

6 apples are in the tree.
A mom picks 2 to give her twins.
How many apples are left for me?

⑤

_____ apples are in the tree!

⑥

4 apples are in the tree.
A girl picks 1 to eat for lunch.
How many apples are left for me?

⑦

_____ apples are in the tree!

⑧

3 apples are in the tree.
A farmer picks 2 to feed his pig.
How many apples are left for me?

⑨

_____ apple is left for me.

⑩

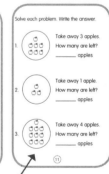

Solve each problem. Write the answer.

1. Take away 3 apples.
    How many are left?
    _____ apples

2. Take away 1 apple.
    How many are left?
    _____ apples

3. Take away 4 apples.
    How many are left?
    _____ apples

⑪

Solve each problem. Write the answer.

Taking It Further

Bring in several different kinds of apples for children to explore. Discuss ways in which the apples are similar to each other, such as they have stems, grow on trees, have seeds inside, and have a rounded shape. Then talk about how the apples are different, for example, in size, color, and height. Afterward, cut each kind of apple open and compare how the insides look. If desired, cut the apples into slices or small chunks for children to sample and compare tastes.

10 apples are in the tree.

A baker picks 3 to make a pie.

How many apples are left for me?

Cut & Paste Mini-Books: Around the Year © 2011 by Nancy I. Sanders, Scholastic Teaching Resources (page 16)

Apples in the Tree

by _____

7 apples are in the tree.

A boy picks 1 to give his teacher.

How many apples are left for me?

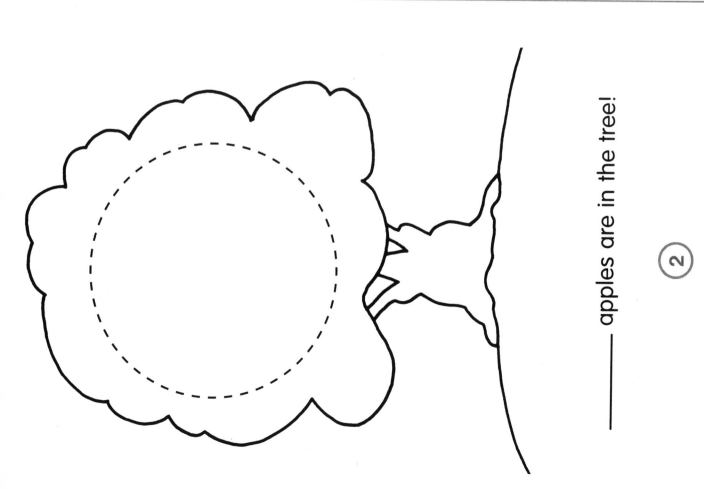

_____ apples are in the tree!

②

6 apples are in the tree.

A mom picks 2 to give her twins.

How many apples are left for me?

Cut & Paste Mini-Books: Around the Year © 2011 by Nancy I. Sanders, Scholastic Teaching Resources (page 18)

⑤

—— apples are in the tree!

④

4 apples are in the tree.

A girl picks 1 to eat for lunch.

How many apples are left for me?

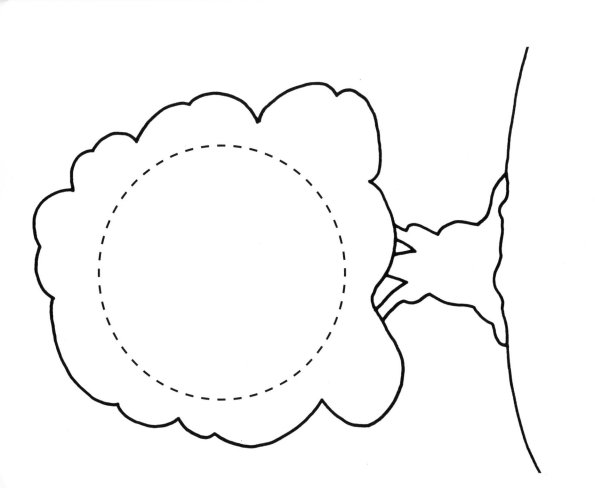

—— apples are in the tree!

⑥

3 apples are in the tree.

A farmer picks 2 to feed his pig.

How many apples are left for me?

—— apples are in the tree!

Solve each problem. Write the answer.

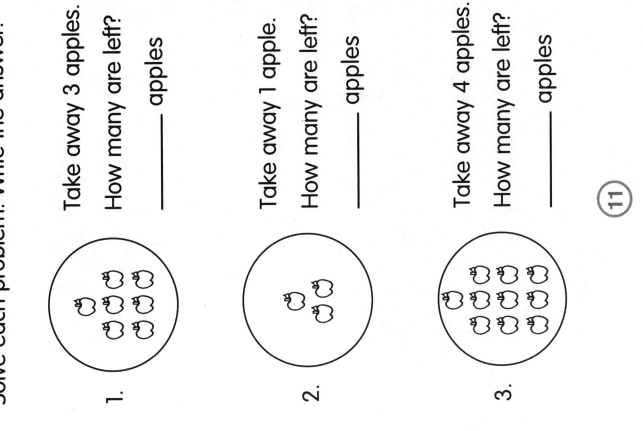

1. Take away 3 apples.
How many are left?

_____ apples

2. Take away 1 apple.
How many are left?

_____ apples

3. Take away 4 apples.
How many are left?

_____ apples

Cut & Paste Mini-Books: Around the Year © 2011 by Nancy I. Sanders, Scholastic Teaching Resources (page 21)

(11)

_____ apple is left for me.

(10)

Apples in the Tree

Cut & Paste Patterns

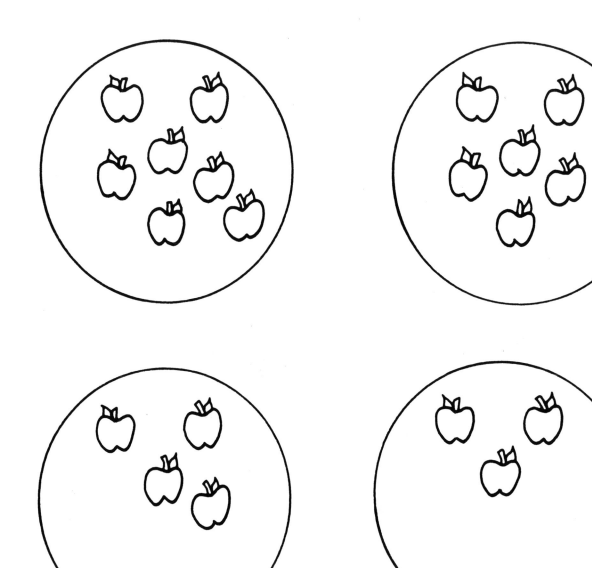

Cut & Paste Mini-Books: Around the Year © 2011 by Nancy I. Sanders, Scholastic Teaching Resources

Pumpkin Time!

Skill Size Concepts

Getting Started

Bring a small and a large pumpkin to class. Help children measure the circumference of each pumpkin, then compare the measurements. You might also have them compare the weights of the two pumpkins. If desired, find pairs of objects around the room in which one item is large and heavy and the other is small and lightweight. Measure and weigh each item in a pair, then have children compare the results.

Completing the Mini-Book

Ask children to write their name on the cover, then cut out and glue the patterns onto the pages, as shown. Finally, have them complete the activity on the last page.

Reproducible Pages
mini-book: pages 24–29
patterns: page 30

Draw a smile on each pumpkin.

Taking It Further

Create a pumpkin-patch word wall to display fall-related words. First, twist lengths of green bulletin board paper to make vines. Attach the vines to a wall and add green leaf cutouts. Then place a basket of orange pumpkin cutouts (in small and large sizes) nearby, along with pencils and clear tape. Invite children to write fall words on the pumpkins and attach them to the vine. They might write "little" words on the small pumpkins and "big" words on the large pumpkins.

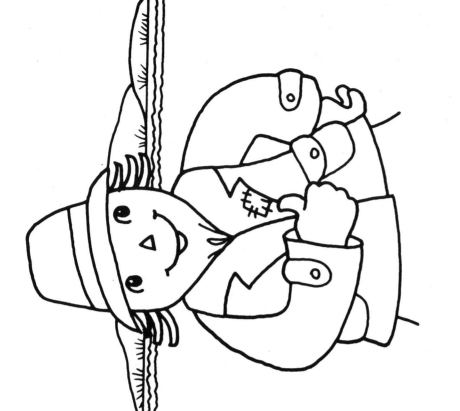

Sam sees a big pumpkin
on a big vine.
He sees a little pumpkin
on a little vine.

Cut & Paste Mini-Books: Around the Year © 2011 by Nancy I. Sanders, Scholastic Teaching Resources (page 24)

Pumpkin Time!

by _____

Sam puts the big pumpkin
in a big basket.
He puts the little pumpkin
in a little basket.

Cut & Paste Mini-Books: Around the Year © 2011 by Nancy I. Sanders, Scholastic Teaching Resources (page 25)

Sam sets the big pumpkin
in a big wagon.
He sets the little pumpkin
in a little wagon.

⑤

Cut & Paste Mini-Books: Around the Year © 2011 by Nancy I. Sanders, Scholastic Teaching Resources (page 26)

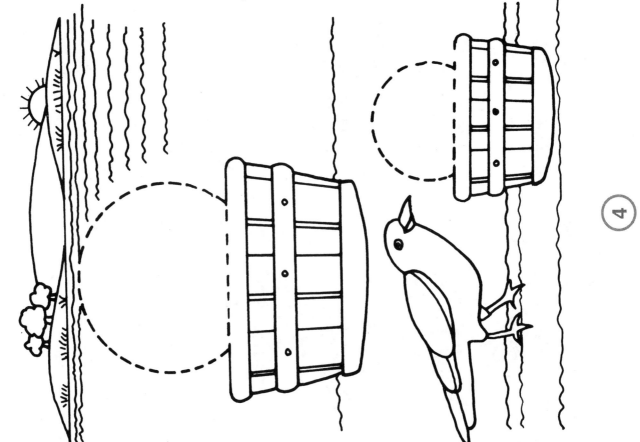

④

Sam sets the big pumpkin
on a big table.
He sets the little pumpkin
on a little table.

⑦

Cut & Paste Mini-Books: Around the Year © 2011 by Nancy I. Sanders, Scholastic Teaching Resources (page 27)

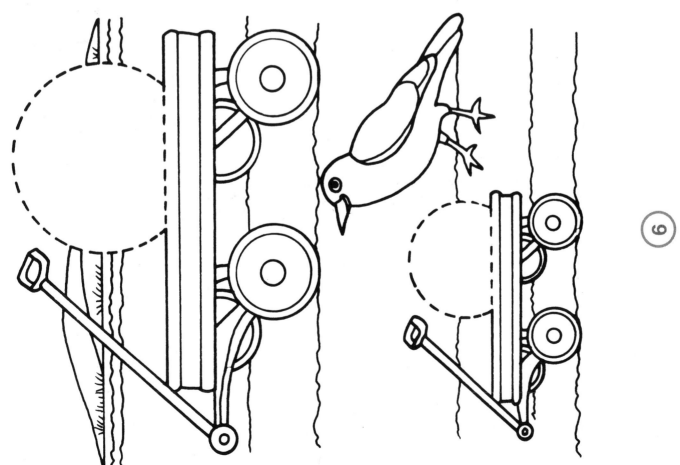

⑥

Sam carves a face
in the big pumpkin.
He carves a face
in the little pumpkin.
Happy Halloween!

Cut & Paste Mini-Books: Around the Year © 2011 by Nancy I. Sanders, Scholastic Teaching Resources (page 28

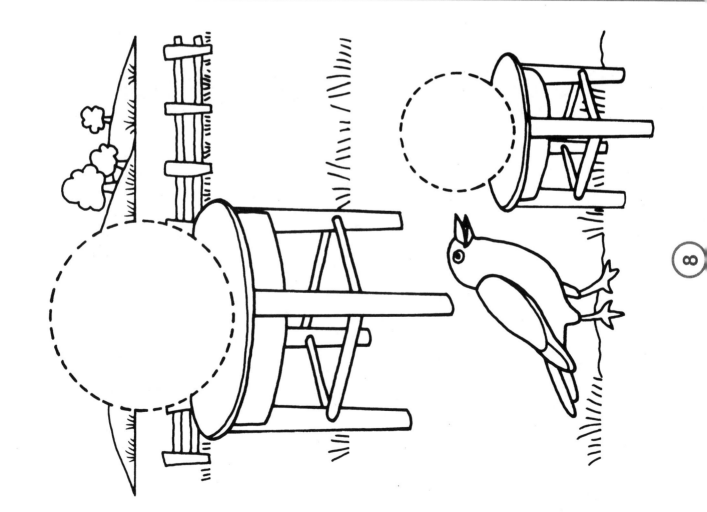

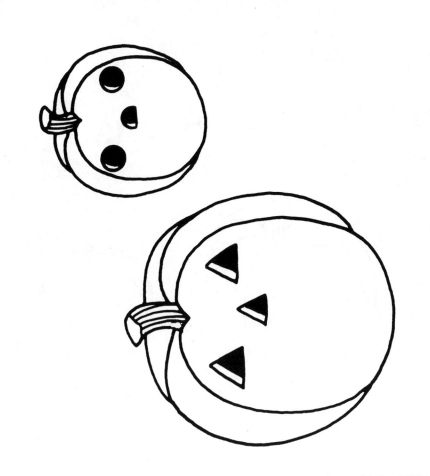

Draw a big smile on the big pumpkin.
Draw a little smile on the little pumpkin.

(11)

Cut & Paste Mini-Books: Around the Year © 2011 by Nancy I. Sanders, Scholastic Teaching Resources (page 29)

(10)

Pumpkin Time!

Cut & Paste Patterns

Cut & Paste Mini-Books: Around the Year © 2011 by Nancy I. Sanders, Scholastic Teaching Resources

Thank You, Squanto

Skill Common Nouns

Getting Started

Invite children to share what they know about how Squanto helped the Pilgrims when they first came to America. As children respond, make a list of common nouns that represent Squanto's help. For example, *berries* might indicate he helped them learn where to find berries, or *friends* might be a reminder that he helped the Pilgrims and Wampanoags become friends. Check that the list includes the bold words on pages 1–9 in the mini-book. When finished, explain that nouns are naming words. Then read the nouns on the list aloud with children, pointing to each one as you say it.

Completing the Mini-Book

Ask children to write their name on the cover, then cut out and glue the patterns onto the pages, as shown. Finally, have them complete the activity on the last page.

Reproducible Pages
mini-book: pages 32–37
patterns: page 38

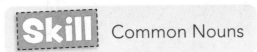

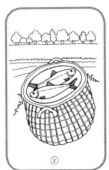

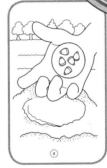

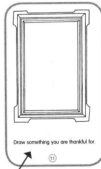

Draw something you are thankful for.

Taking It Further

At the first Thanksgiving, the Pilgrims celebrated an abundant harvest, which was in part possible because of Squanto's help. After sharing this information, invite children to make a class wreath of thanks. First, have them trace their hand onto a sheet of construction paper in a fall color (yellow, orange, brown, and so on). Help them cut out their outline and label it with the name of a person whose help they are thankful for, as well as how that person has been helpful. Use the cutouts to create a large wreath on a class bulletin board for all to enjoy.

Squanto helped the Pilgrims catch **fish**.

"Thank you," they said to Squanto.

"Thank you."

Cut & Paste Mini-Books: Around the Year © 2011 by Nancy I. Sanders, Scholastic Teaching Resources (page 32

Thank You, Squanto

by _____

Squanto helped the Pilgrims plant **seeds**.

"Thank you," they said to Squanto.

"Thank you."

③

Cut & Paste Mini-Books: Around the Year © 2011 by Nancy I. Sanders, Scholastic Teaching Resources (page 33)

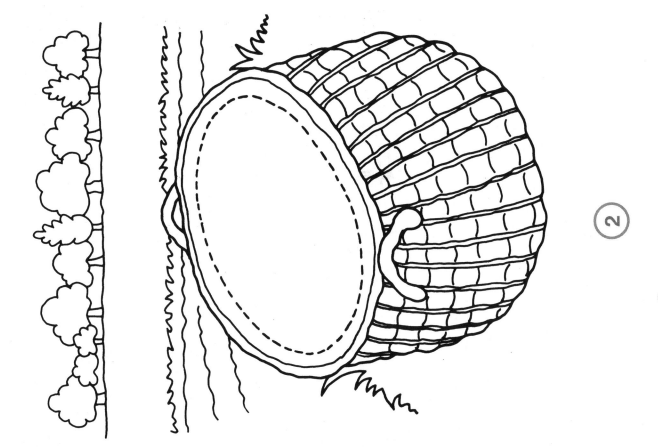

②

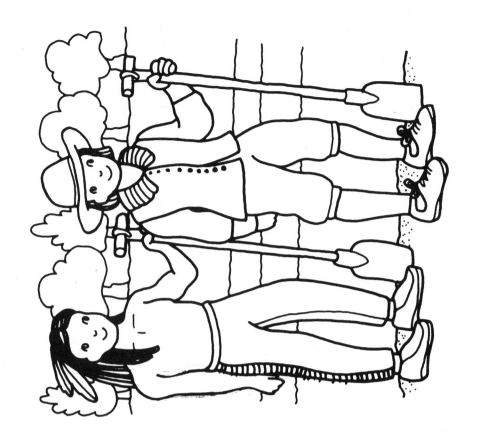

Squanto helped the Pilgrims grow **corn.**

"Thank you," they said to Squanto.

"Thank you."

Cut & Paste Mini-Books: Around the Year © 2011 by Nancy I. Sanders, Scholastic Teaching Resources (page 34

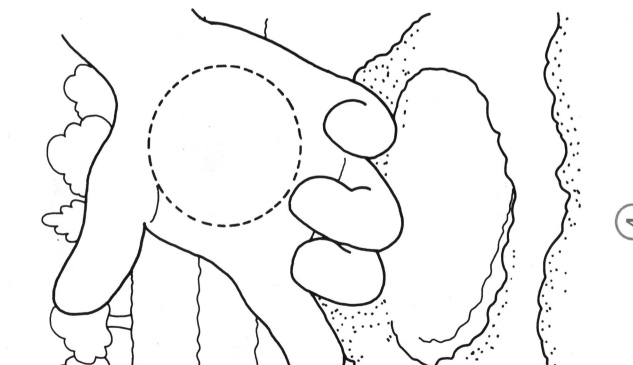

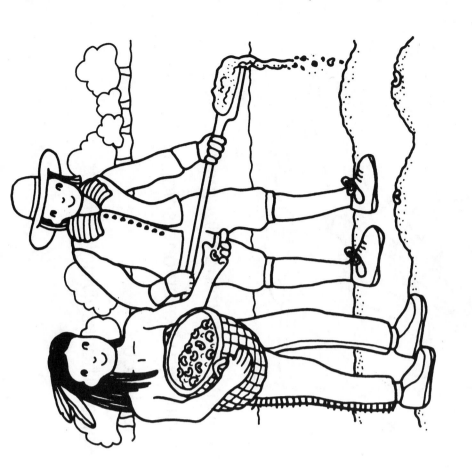

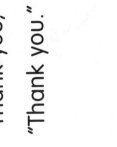

Squanto helped the Pilgrims grow **beans**.

"Thank you," they said to Squanto.

"Thank you."

⑦

Cut & Paste Mini-Books: Around the Year © 2011 by Nancy I. Sanders, Scholastic Teaching Resources (page 35)

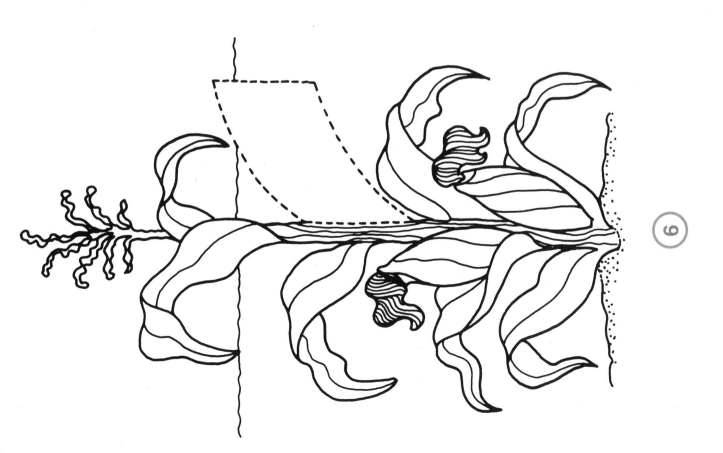

⑥

Squanto helped the Pilgrims eat **food**.

"Thank you," everyone said.

"Thank you."

Happy Thanksgiving!

Cut & Paste Mini-Books: Around the Year © 2011 by Nancy I. Sanders, Scholastic Teaching Resources (page 36)

⑥

⑧

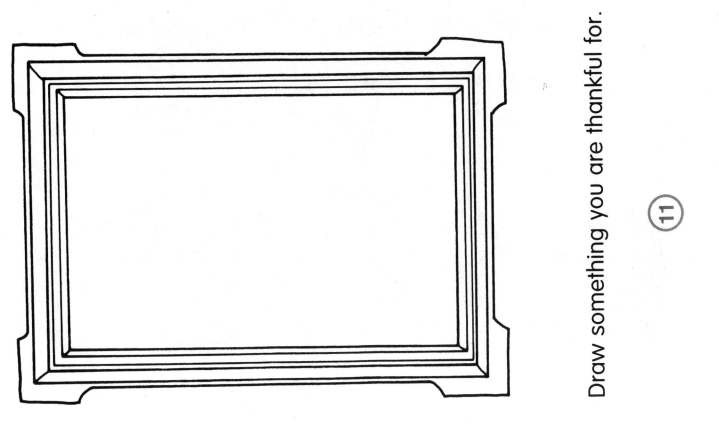

Draw something you are thankful for.

(11)

Cut & Paste Mini-Books: Around the Year © 2011 by Nancy I. Sanders, Scholastic Teaching Resources (page 37)

(10)

Thank You, Squanto

Cut & Paste Patterns

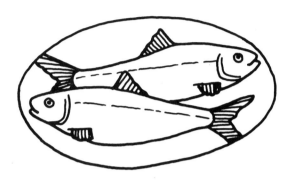

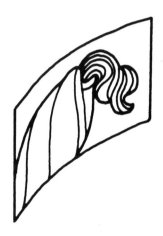
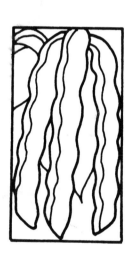

Cut & Paste Mini-Books: Around the Year © 2011 by Nancy I. Sanders, Scholastic Teaching Resources

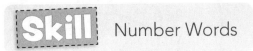

Winter Is Here!

Skill Number Words

Getting Started

Display five or more die-cut snowflakes on the chalkboard. (Attach them with removable adhesive.) Then write each number word for 1 to 5 on separate index cards. To use, give a child a word card. Ask the child to read the word aloud, then remove that many snowflakes from the board. Was the child's response correct? After checking with the class, have the child return the snowflakes to the display. Continue until every child has had a turn to read a number word and remove the corresponding number of snowflakes from the board.

Completing the Mini-Book

Ask children to write their name on the cover, then cut out and glue the patterns onto the pages, as shown. Finally, have them complete the activity on the last page.

Reproducible Pages
mini-book: pages 40–45
patterns: page 46

Winter Is Here!
by _____

One pretty snowflake falls on my hat.
①

②

Two pretty snowflakes fall on my cat.
③

④

Three pretty snowflakes fall on my feet.
⑤

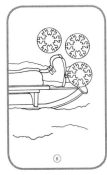
⑥

Four pretty snowflakes fall on the street.
⑦

⑧

Five pretty snowflakes fall in the air.
Snowflakes, snowflakes, everywhere!
⑨

⑩

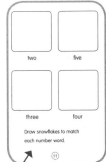
two   five

three   four

Draw snowflakes to match each number word.
⑪

Draw snowflakes to match each number word.

Taking It Further

Use blue and white paper to create a simple outdoor scene of a sky and snow-covered ground. At the top, add the title "Signs of Winter." Then brainstorm with children a list of things they might see in winter that signifies the season. Their responses might include snowfall, ice-skaters, snowmen, icicles, hibernating bears, and so on. Afterward, invite children to draw, cut out, and add their own pictures to the scene to depict signs of winter.

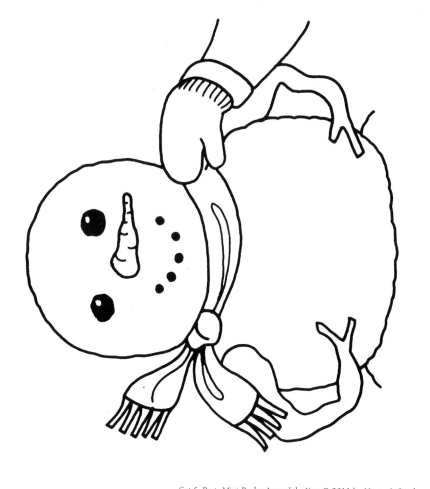

One pretty snowflake falls on my hat.

Winter Is Here!

by _____

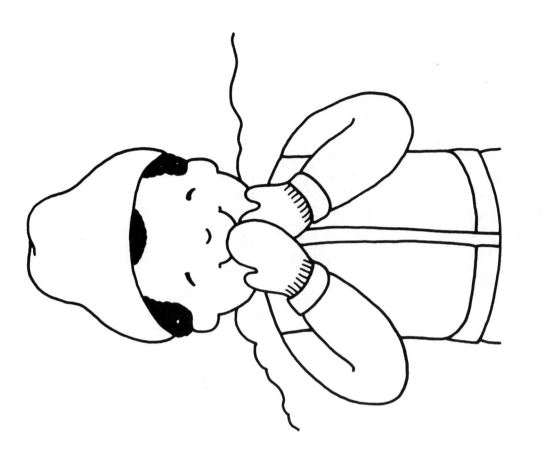

Two pretty snowflakes fall on my cat.

③

Cut & Paste Mini-Books: Around the Year © 2011 by Nancy I. Sanders, Scholastic Teaching Resources (page 41)

②

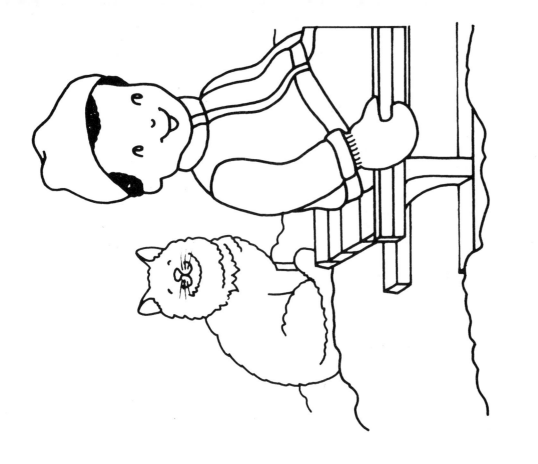

Three pretty snowflakes fall on my feet.

5

Cut & Paste Mini-Books: Around the Year © 2011 by Nancy I. Sanders, Scholastic Teaching Resources (page 42)

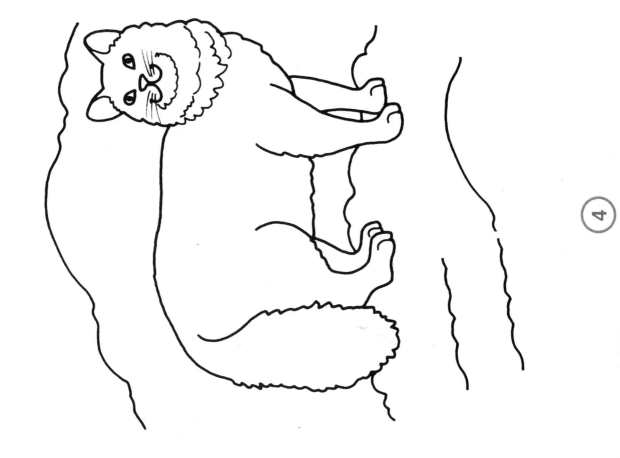

4

Four pretty snowflakes fall on the street.

7

Cut & Paste Mini-Books: Around the Year © 2011 by Nancy I. Sanders, Scholastic Teaching Resources (page 43)

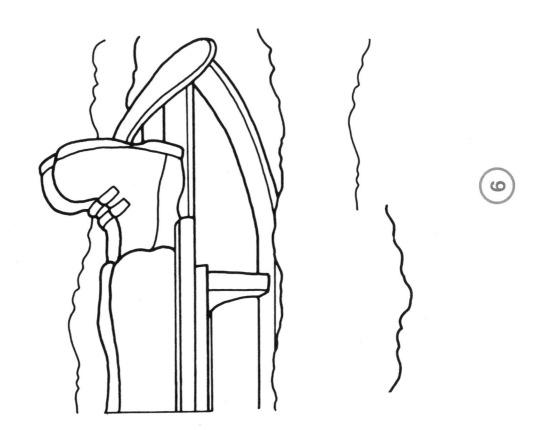

6

Five pretty snowflakes fall in the air.
Snowflakes, snowflakes, everywhere!

Cut & Paste Mini-Books: Around the Year © 2011 by Nancy I. Sanders, Scholastic Teaching Resources (page 44)

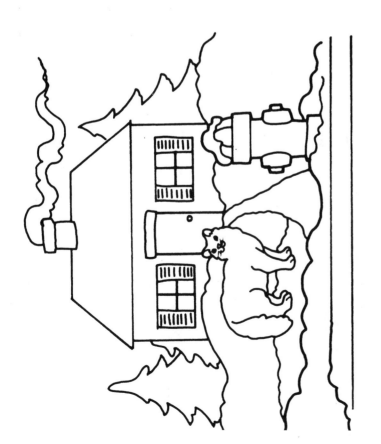

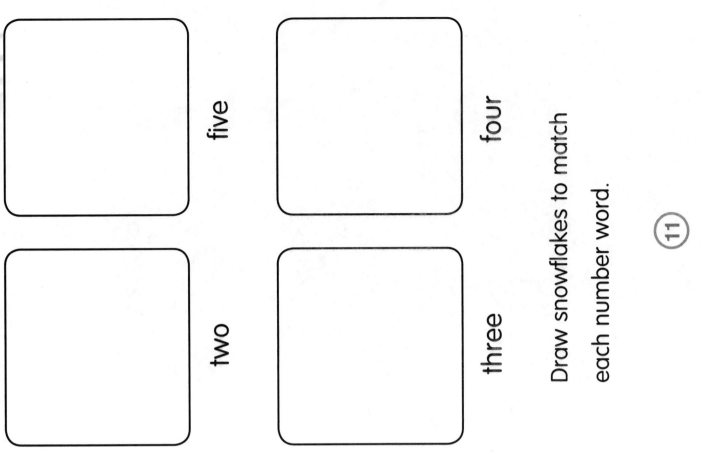

five

four

two

three

Draw snowflakes to match each number word.

⑪

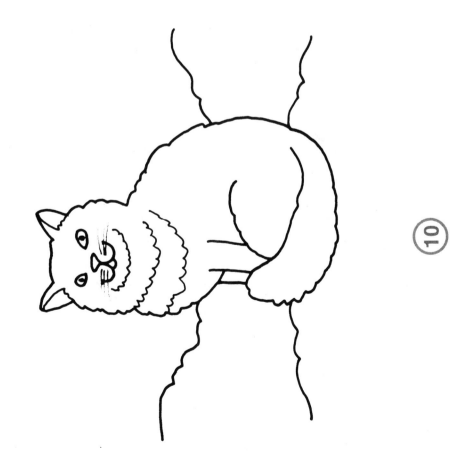

⑩

Winter Is Here!

Cut & Paste Patterns

Cut & Paste Mini-Books: Around the Year © 2011 by Nancy I. Sanders, Scholastic Teaching Resources

A Colorful Holiday

Getting Started

Prepare die-cut shapes that correspond to several items in the mini-book, such as a candle, gift, ball, and cupcake. Cut the shapes from different colors of construction paper including red, blue, yellow, green, and purple. Display the cutouts on a bulletin board or on the chalkboard tray. Write each color word on a separate index card and put the cards in a paper bag. To use, have children draw a card from the bag, read the color word, then find a cutout that matches the color. When finished, have them return the word card to the bag.

Completing the Mini-Book

Ask children to write their name on the cover, then cut out and glue the patterns onto the pages, as shown. Finally, have them complete the activity on the last page.

> **Reproducible Pages**
> mini-book:
> pages 48–53
> patterns: page 54

A Colorful Holiday

by _____

Holiday lights are a pretty sight.
This blue candle shines so bright.

①

Color the candle **blue**.

②

Here are gifts for all to see.
This big purple gift is just for me!

③

Color the gift **purple**.

④

New toys and games cover the floor.
My yellow ball is by the door.

⑤

Color the ball **yellow**.

⑥

This table is full of yummy treats.
I'll choose a green cupcake to eat.

⑦

Color the cupcake **green**.

⑧

After such a fun and busy day,
my red quilt helps me dream away.

⑨

Color the quilt **red**.

⑩

red   green

blue

purple   yellow

Color each candle.

⑪

> **Color each candle.**

Taking It Further

Invite children to bring in a photo that shows how they celebrate a winter holiday. Have them attach the photo to the top half of a sheet of paper, then draw their favorite thing about that holiday on the bottom half. (If children are unable to provide a photo, they may illustrate both sections of the paper.) When finished, assemble all the pages into a class book titled "Our Holiday Photo Album." Share the album with the class, inviting children to tell about their own page. Then add the book to your class library.

Holiday lights are a pretty sight.

This blue candle shines so bright.

Cut & Paste Mini-Books: Around the Year © 2011 by Nancy I. Sanders, Scholastic Teaching Resources (page 48)

A Colorful Holiday

Happy •••• Holidays

by _____

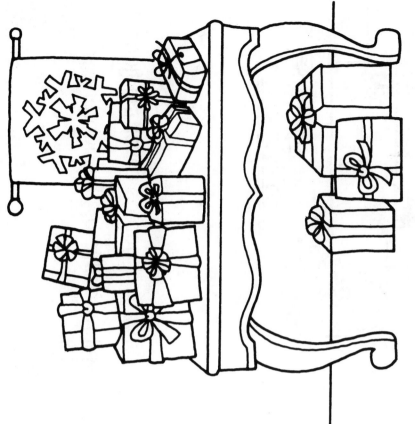

Here are gifts for all to see.

This big purple gift is just for me!

③

Cut & Paste Mini-Books: Around the Year © 2011 by Nancy I. Sanders, Scholastic Teaching Resources (page 49)

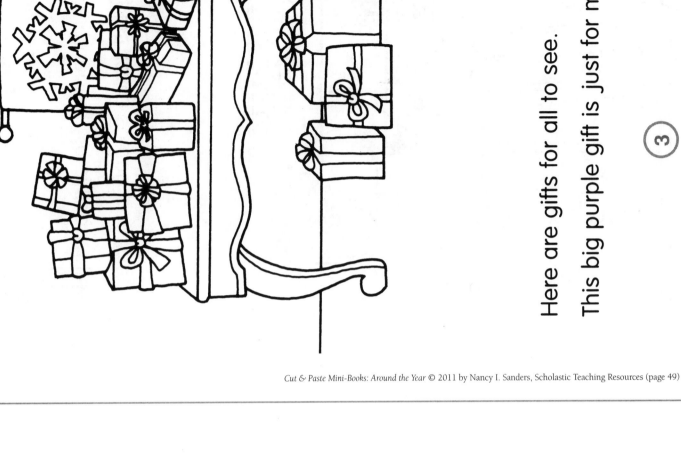

Color the candle **blue**.

②

New toys and games cover the floor.

My yellow ball is by the door.

Cut & Paste Mini-Books: Around the Year © 2011 by Nancy I. Sanders, Scholastic Teaching Resources (page 50)

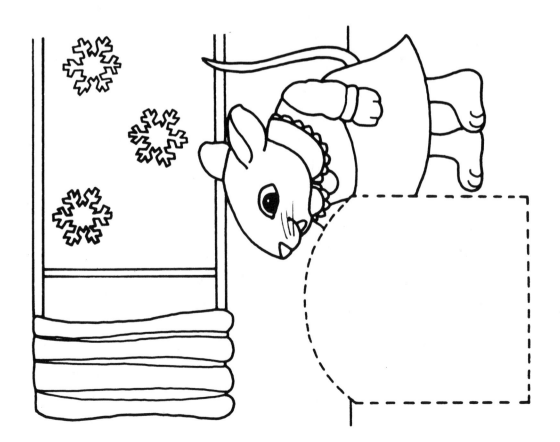

Color the gift **purple**.

4

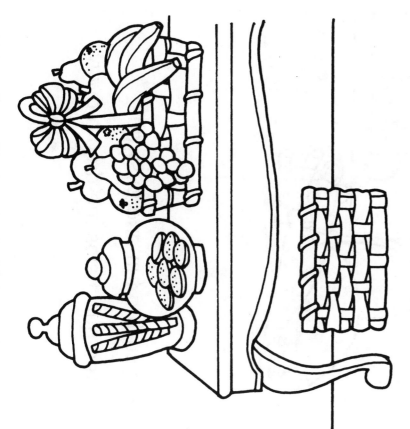

This table is full of yummy treats.

I'll choose a green cupcake to eat.

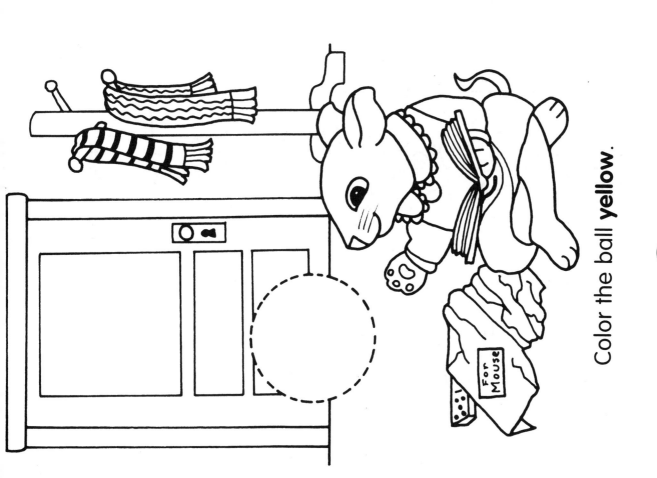

Color the ball **yellow**.

6

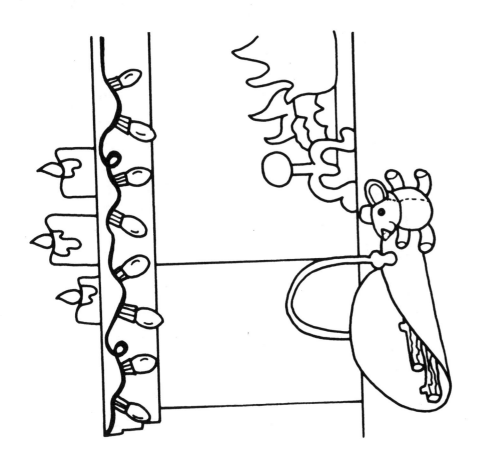

After such a fun and busy day,
my red quilt helps me dream away.

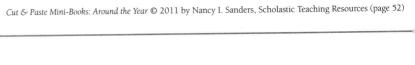

⑨

Cut & Paste Mini-Books: Around the Year © 2011 by Nancy I. Sanders, Scholastic Teaching Resources (page 52)

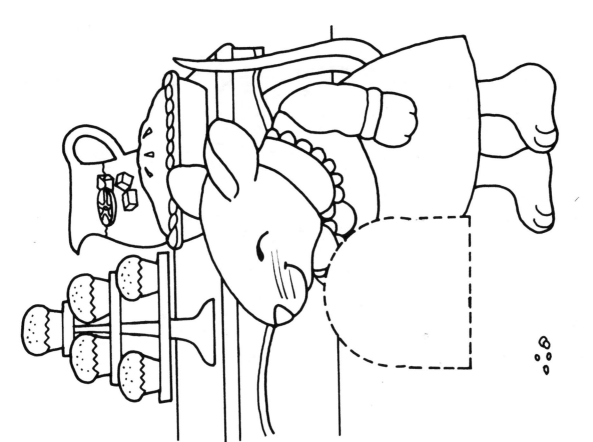

Color the cupcake **green.**

⑧

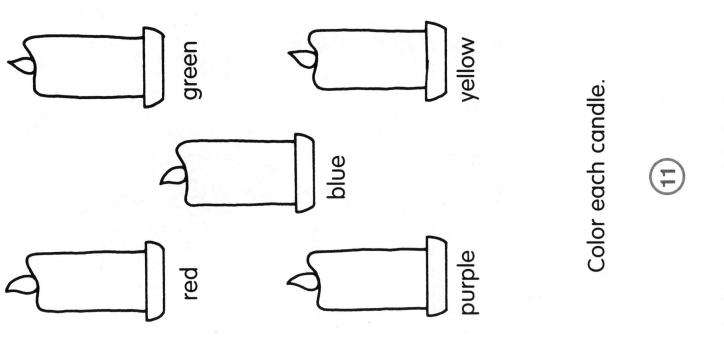

green

yellow

blue

red

purple

Color each candle.

(11)

Cut & Paste Mini-Books: Around the Year © 2011 by Nancy I. Sanders, Scholastic Teaching Resources (page 53)

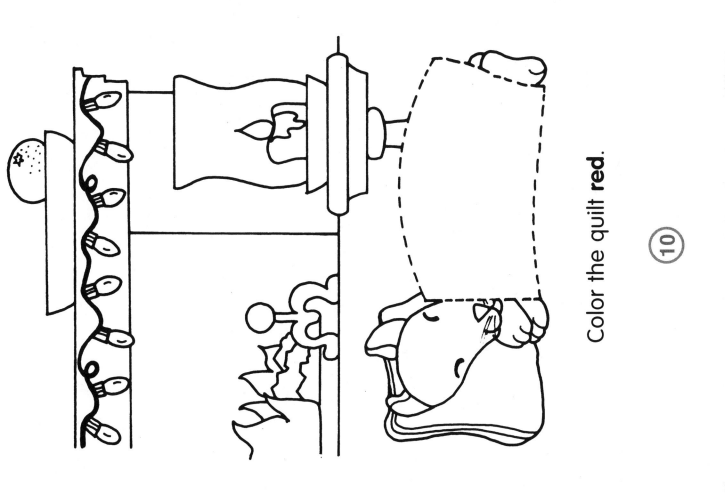

Color the quilt **red**.

(10)

A Colorful Holiday

Cut & Paste Patterns

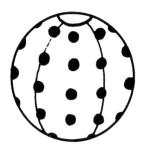

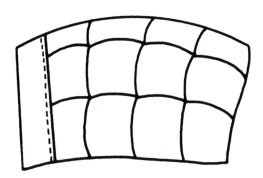

Cut & Paste Mini-Books: Around the Year © 2011 by Nancy I. Sanders, Scholastic Teaching Resources

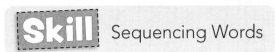

New Year's Day Parade

Getting Started

Arrange five or six different plastic farm animals in a line. Point out the front of the line, then ask children to tell which animal is first. After they respond, have them name the animal that's next, and then last. To continue, name a specific animal in the line and have children name the animal that comes after that one. Rearrange the animals and repeat the activity, using sequencing words such as *first, next, last,* and *after.*

Completing the Mini-Book

Ask children to write their name on the cover, then cut out and glue the patterns onto the pages, as shown. Finally, have them complete the activity on the last page.

Reproducible Pages
mini-book:
pages 56–61
patterns: page 62

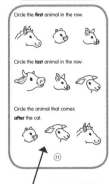

Circle the animal in each row to show its position.

Taking It Further

Have a class New Year's Day parade! Give children plain party hats to decorate with paper cutouts, glitter, ribbon, stickers, scraps of foil, and other craft materials. When finished, work with children to write a special New Year's cheer. Then invite children to don their festive hats, line up, and march around the room to some lively music. Periodically, stop the music and rearrange children's positions in line so that a different child is first or last. Finally, recite the class cheer to wish everyone a happy New Year!

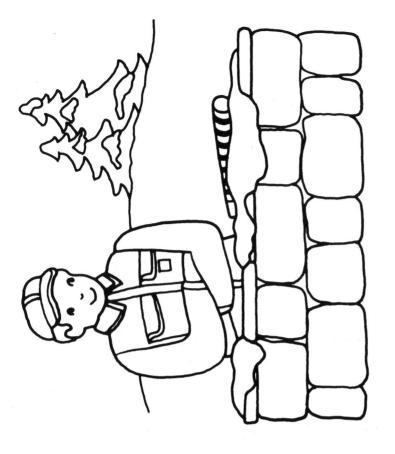

Here comes the New Year's Day

parade on the farm!

First comes the cat

with a bird on her hat.

1

Cut & Paste Mini-Books: Around the Year © 2011 by Nancy I. Sanders, Scholastic Teaching Resources (page 56)

New Year's Day Parade

by _____

Next comes the pig
wearing a hat and wig.

③

Cut & Paste Mini-Books: Around the Year © 2011 by Nancy I. Sanders, Scholastic Teaching Resources (page 57)

②

Then comes the horse
in a cowboy hat, of course!

⑤

Cut & Paste Mini-Books: Around the Year © 2011 by Nancy I. Sanders, Scholastic Teaching Resources (page 58)

④

After that comes the sheep
with a hat that goes "Beep!"

⑦

Cut & Paste Mini-Books: Around the Year © 2011 by Nancy I. Sanders, Scholastic Teaching Resources (page 59)

⑥

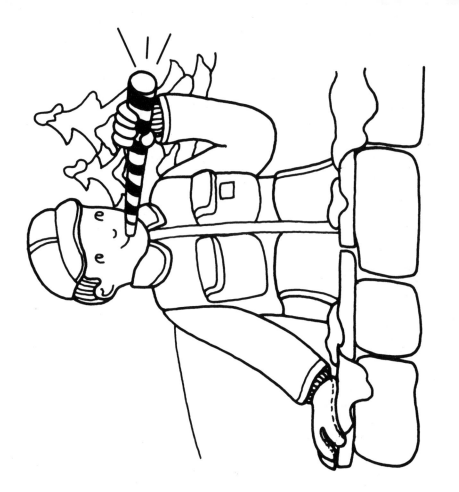

And the cow comes **last**.

Her hat is a blast!

Happy New Year!

(9)

Cut & Paste Mini-Books: Around the Year © 2011 by Nancy I. Sanders, Scholastic Teaching Resources (page 60)

(8)

Circle the **first** animal in the row.

Circle the **last** animal in the row.

Circle the animal that comes **after** the cat.

Cut & Paste Mini-Books: Around the Year © 2011 by Nancy I. Sanders, Scholastic Teaching Resources (page 61)

11

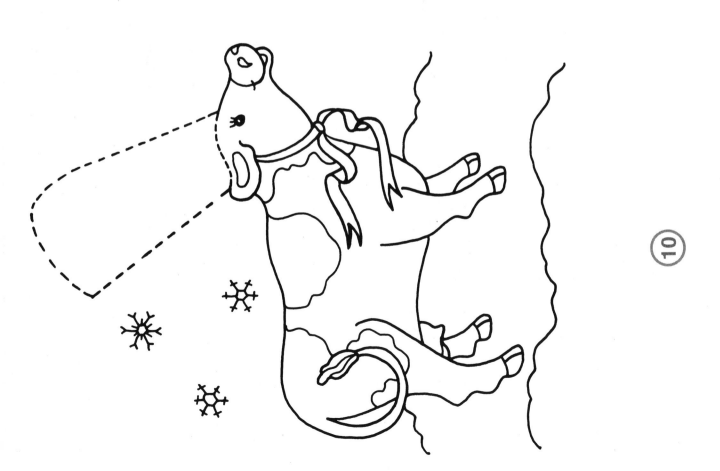

10

New Year's Day Parade

Cut & Paste Patterns

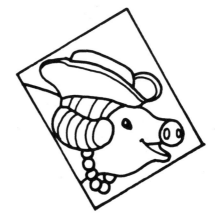

Cut & Paste Mini-Books: Around the Year © 2011 by Nancy I. Sanders, Scholastic Teaching Resources

Dr. King Had a Dream

Getting Started

Tell children that Dr. Martin Luther King, Jr., had a vision that all people would be treated equally and live peacefully together. Connect his dream of friendship for all with this counting activity. First, seat children in a circle on the floor. Then say, "I have a dream that ___ kids will be friends." Fill in the blank with a number from 1 to 10. Next, name a child to go around the circle and tap that many children. Ask those children to stand, then have the class count them to check that the number standing equals the number stated. Finally, have everyone take a seat for another round of play.

Completing the Mini-Book

Ask children to write their name on the cover, then cut out and glue the patterns onto the pages, as shown. Finally, have them complete the activity on the last page.

Reproducible Pages
mini-book: pages 64–69
patterns: pages 70–71

Dr. King Had a Dream
ALL ABOUT Dr. Martin Luther King, Jr.
by ___

2 little children walking hand in hand—Dr. King had a dream of freedom in our land.
①

②

Burger Menu
4 little children sitting side by side—Dr. King had a dream of being friends with pride.
③

④

6 little children riding on the bus—Dr. King had a dream of peace for all of us.
⑤

School Bus
⑥

8 little children with their soccer ball—Dr. King had a dream of equal rights for all.
⑦

10 little children learning something new—Dr. King had a dream that one day would come true!
⑧

Dr. King's Dream
⑨

Dr. Martin Luther King, Jr., said, "Let freedom ring!"
⑩

I have a dream.
Trace the letters. Read the words.
⑪

Trace the letters. Read the words.

Taking It Further

Share a picture book or two with children to help them learn more about Dr. King. Some titles you might read include *A Picture Book of Martin Luther King, Jr.,* by David A. Adler, *Happy Birthday, Martin Luther King, Jr.,* by Jean Marzollo, and *Martin's Big Words: The Life of Dr. Martin Luther King, Jr.,* by Doreen Rappaport. Afterward, invite children to share ways they might follow Dr. King's example in helping to make a difference in their home, school, community, and world.

Dr. King Had a Dream

ALL ABOUT
Dr. Martin Luther King, Jr.

by _____

---

2 little children walking hand in hand—

Dr. King had a dream of freedom

in our land.

Yum Burger says Welcome!

Burger Menu
Single Burger 2.00
Cheese Burger 2.50
Double Burger 3.00
Bacon Burger 3.50

4 little children sitting side by side—

Dr. King had a dream of being friends

with pride.

③

Cut & Paste Mini-Books: Around the Year © 2011 by Nancy I. Sanders, Scholastic Teaching Resources (page 65)

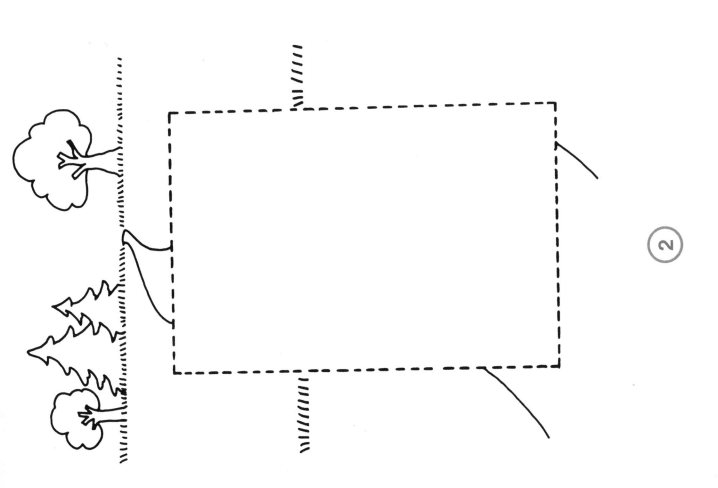

②

6 little children riding on the bus—
Dr. King had a dream of peace
for all of us.

(5)

Cut & Paste Mini-Books: Around the Year © 2011 by Nancy I. Sanders, Scholastic Teaching Resources (page 66

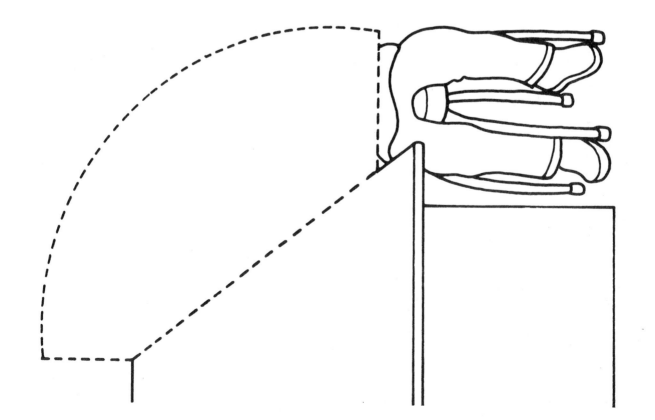

(4)

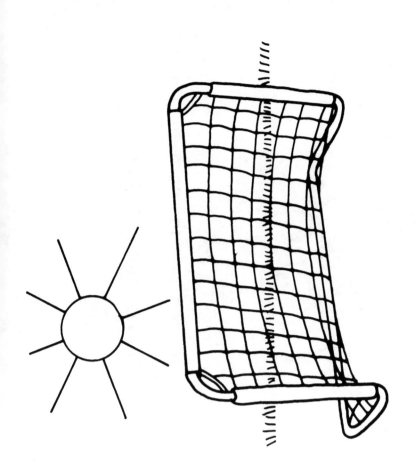

8 little children with their soccer ball—

Dr. King had a dream of equal rights for all.

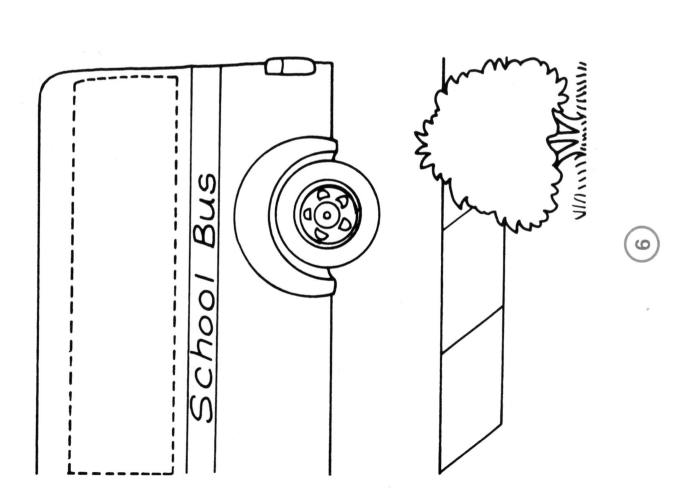

6

Dr. King's Dream

10 little children learning something new—

Dr. King had a dream that one day would come true!

Cut & Paste Mini-Books: Around the Year © 2011 by Nancy I. Sanders, Scholastic Teaching Resources (page 68)

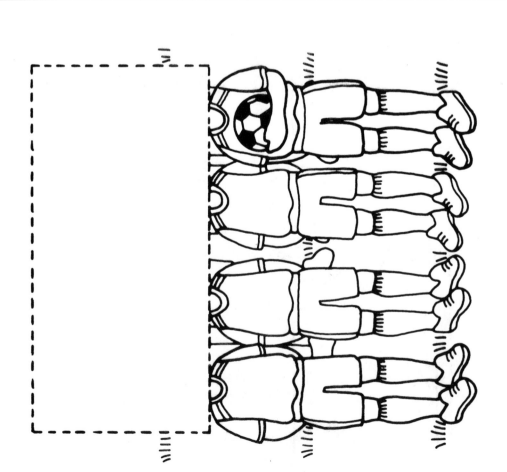

I have a dream.

Trace the letters. Read the words.

Cut & Paste Mini-Books: Around the Year © 2011 by Nancy I. Sanders, Scholastic Teaching Resources (page 69)

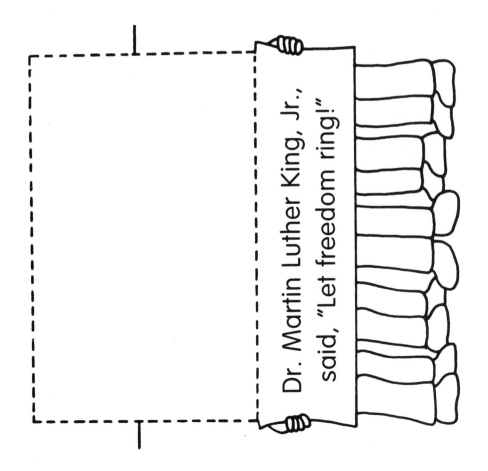

Dr. Martin Luther King, Jr., said, "Let freedom ring!"

Dr. King Had a Dream

Cut & Paste Patterns

Cut & Paste Mini-Books: Around the Year © 2011 by Nancy I. Sanders, Scholastic Teaching Resources

Dr. King Had a Dream

Cut & Paste Patterns

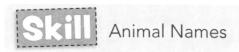

Presidential Pets

Skill Animal Names

Getting Started

Tell children that many presidents had pets while living in the White House. In addition to common pets like dogs, cats, and birds, some presidents had interesting or unusual pets—even the kind that might be found in a zoo! Invite children to brainstorm a list of animals that might have been presidents' pets. Include these animal names on the list: *pony, hippo, zebra, turkey,* and *alligator.* Afterward, highlight those five animals, then point to and name each one several times, inviting children to read the word with you. Finally, tell children that they will make a book about presidents who kept these animals as pets in the White House.

Completing the Mini-Book

Ask children to write their name on the cover, then cut out and glue the patterns onto the pages, as shown. Finally, have them complete the activity on the last page.

Reproducible Pages
mini-book:
pages 73–78
patterns: page 79

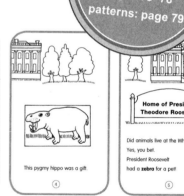

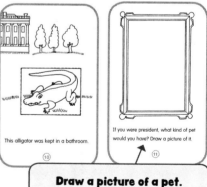

Draw a picture of a pet.

Taking It Further

For Presidents' Day, visit www.presidentialpetmuseum.com/whitehousepets-1.htm for a fun and interesting way to familiarize children with the names of all the United States Presidents—and their pets! Here, you can find a list that includes each president, his years in office, and the pets his family owned during his presidency. Afterward, invite children to write about and illustrate a pet they might like to have at the White House, if they were president.

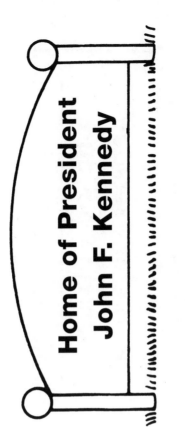

Home of President
John F. Kennedy

Did animals live at the White House?

Yes, you bet.

President Kennedy

had a **pony** for a pet!

Cut & Paste Mini-Books: Around the Year © 2011 by Nancy I. Sanders, Scholastic Teaching Resources (page 73)

Presidential
Pets

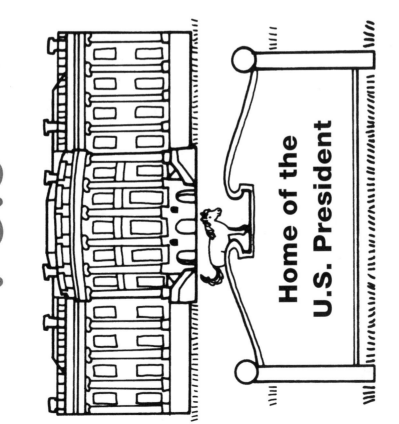

Home of the
U.S. President

by _____

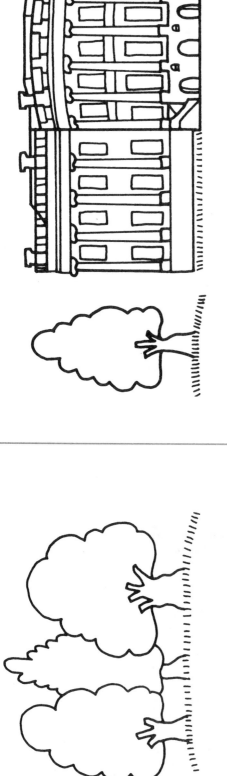

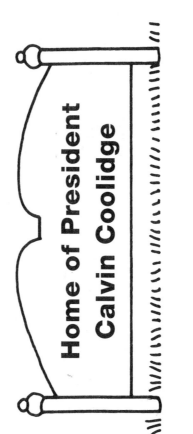

Home of President Calvin Coolidge

Did animals live at the White House?

Yes, you bet.

President Coolidge

had a **hippo** for a pet!

Cut & Paste Mini-Books: Around the Year © 2011 by Nancy I. Sanders, Scholastic Teaching Resources (page 74)

This pony was named Macaroni.

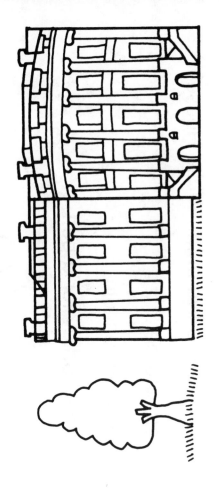

Home of President Theodore Roosevelt

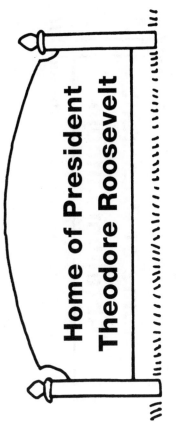

Did animals live at the White House?

Yes, you bet.

President Roosevelt had a **zebra** for a **pet**!

⑤

Cut & Paste Mini-Books: Around the Year © 2011 by Nancy I. Sanders, Scholastic Teaching Resources (page 75)

This pygmy hippo was a gift.

 ④

Home of President Abraham Lincoln

Did animals live at the White House?

Yes, you bet.

President Lincoln
had a **turkey** for a pet!

⑦

This zebra was sent from Africa.

⑥

Home of President John Quincy Adams

Did animals live at the White House?

Yes, you bet.

President Adams

had an **alligator** for a pet!

⑨

Cut & Paste Mini-Books: Around the Year © 2011 by Nancy I. Sanders, Scholastic Teaching Resources (page 77)

This turkey was named Jack.

⑧

If you were president, what kind of pet would you have? Draw a picture of it.

Cut & Paste Mini-Books: Around the Year © 2011 by Nancy I. Sanders, Scholastic Teaching Resources (page 78)

11

This alligator was kept in a bathroom.

10

Presidential Pets

Cut & Paste Patterns

My Special Valentines

Getting Started

Cut out a large circle, square, triangle, rectangle, diamond, and heart. Use removable adhesive to attach each shape to the left side of the chalkboard. Write each shape name in random order on the right. Point to each shape and ask children to name it. Talk about the attributes of that shape, such as the number of sides and corners it has. Then invite a volunteer to find the matching word and draw a line from the shape to its name. When finished, erase the lines, rearrange the shapes, and repeat the activity.

Completing the Mini-Book

Ask children to write their name on the cover, then cut out and glue the patterns onto the pages, as shown. Finally, have them complete the activity on the last page.

Reproducible Pages
mini-book: pages 81–86
patterns: pages 87–88

My mom is loving. She is always there. This **circle** valentine tells her I care.

①

My friend is silly and likes to pretend. This **square** valentine is the one I'll send.

②

③

④

My teacher is special. He's so smart and fun. This **triangle** valentine says he's number one!

⑤

⑥

My grandpa is jolly. He laughs all the time! This **rectangle** valentine has a funny rhyme.

⑦

⑧

My sister is great. She's friendly and sweet. This **diamond** valentine has a special treat.

⑨

⑩

Connect the dots. What shape did you make? A _____ !

⑪

Connect the dots. Write the name of the shape.

Taking It Further

Invite children to create valentines from a variety of shapes. First, provide large shape cutouts that include circles, squares, triangles, rectangles, diamonds, and hearts as well as other shapes, such as ovals, pentagons, and octagons. After reviewing the name of each shape, have children choose a shape to use as a valentine. They might draw a funny valentine picture or write a sweet message for someone special, such as a friend, parent, family member, or school worker. When finished, encourage children to present their valentines to their chosen recipients.

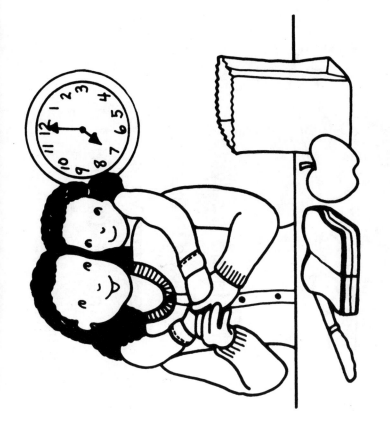

My mom is loving.

She is always there.

This **circle** valentine

tells her I care.

My Special Valentines

Make
**valentines
for my**
☐ Mom
☐ Best friend
☐ Teacher
☐ Grandpa
☐ Sister

by _____

My friend is silly
and likes to pretend.
This **square** valentine
is the one I'll send.

③

Cut & Paste Mini-Books: Around the Year © 2011 by Nancy I. Sanders, Scholastic Teaching Resources (page 82)

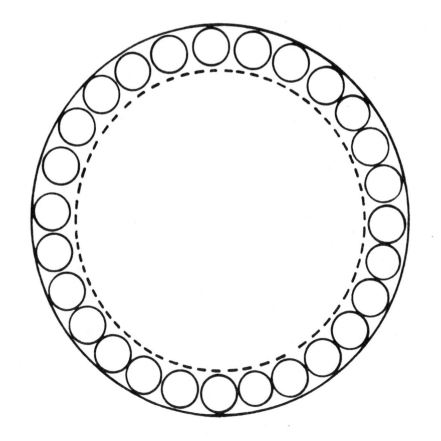

②

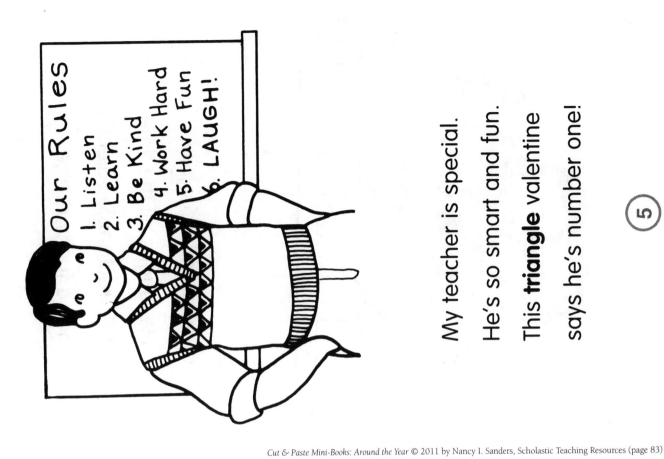

My teacher is special.

He's so smart and fun.

This **triangle** valentine

says he's number one!

Cut & Paste Mini-Books: Around the Year © 2011 by Nancy I. Sanders, Scholastic Teaching Resources (page 83)

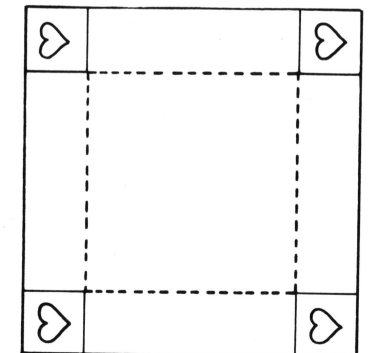

My grandpa is jolly.

He laughs all the time!

This **rectangle** valentine

has a funny rhyme.

⑦

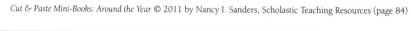
Cut & Paste Mini-Books: Around the Year © 2011 by Nancy I. Sanders, Scholastic Teaching Resources (page 84)

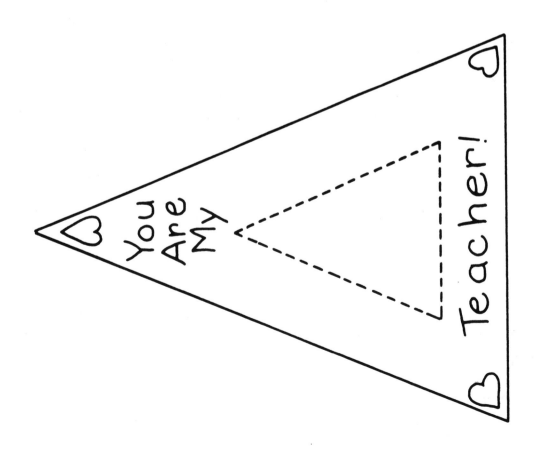

You Are My

Teacher!

⑥

My sister is great.

She's friendly and sweet.

This **diamond** valentine

has a special treat.

⑧

Happy
Valentine's
Day

2
3
1
4
10
5
9
6
8
7

Connect the dots.
What shape did you make?

A _____ !

Cut & Paste Mini-Books: Around the Year © 2011 by Nancy I. Sanders, Scholastic Teaching Resources (page 8

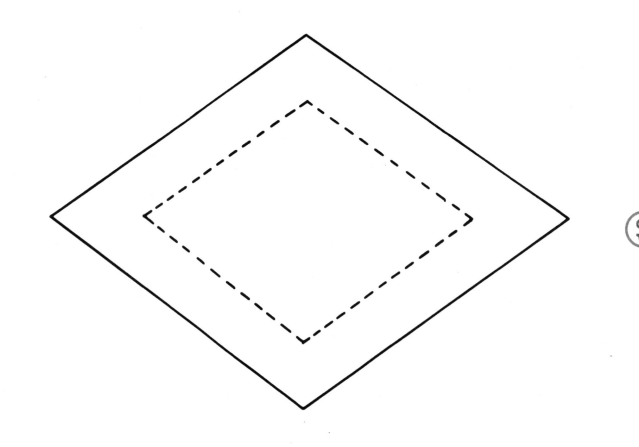

My Special Valentines

Cut & Paste Patterns

Cut & Paste Patterns

Funny Grandpa

👁 love **U**.

You **R** sweet

and Silly **2**!

We ♥ to

LAUGH,

both **U** and 👁.

Grandpa,

you're my favorite

Guy!

Cut & Paste Mini-Books: Around the Year © 2011 by Nancy I. Sanders, Scholastic Teaching Resources

Hello, Spring!

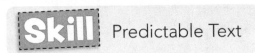

Skill   Predictable Text

Getting Started

Walk outdoors with children on a nice, spring day. Point out some signs of spring, such as sprouting plants, budding leaves, and bird nests. While enjoying nature, help children make predictions about the progression of a plant's growth, or the activity that occurs in a bird's nest. For example, point out a branch that has a leaf bud and say, "Here is a tree that grows a branch, and on that branch grows a ____." Guide children to complete the sentence with *bud*. Then continue with "And from that bud grows a ____." (*leaf*).

Completing the Mini-Book

Ask children to write their name on the cover, then cut out and glue the patterns onto the pages, as shown. Finally, have them complete the activity on the last page.

> **Reproducible Pages**
> mini-book: pages 90–95
> patterns: page 96

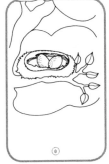

Circle the things that are seen in spring.

Taking It Further

Make a word-family tree to feature spring-related words. Use long and short pieces of twisted brown bulletin board paper to create the trunk and branches. Attach the tree to a wall, then label green leaf cutouts with words such as *tree, seed, plant, nest, egg, hatch,* and *grow*. Attach each word to a different branch. Then invite children to label additional leaves with words belonging to the same word families as the words on the tree. Have them attach the leaves to the corresponding branch. Later, encourage children to use words from the tree in their creative writing about spring.

One fine day,
I sat in my tree.
And on that tree
I saw a branch.
Hello, branch!

Cut & Paste Mini-Books: Around the Year © 2011 by Nancy I. Sanders, Scholastic Teaching Resources (page 90)

Hello, Spring!

by _____

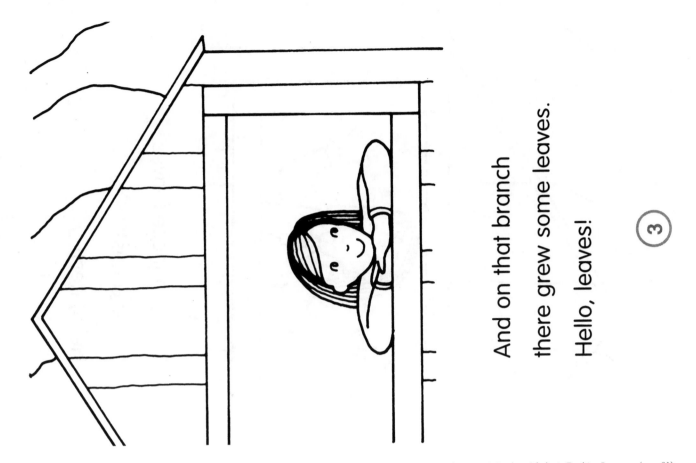

And on that branch
there grew some leaves.
Hello, leaves!

③

Cut & Paste Mini-Books: Around the Year © 2011 by Nancy I. Sanders, Scholastic Teaching Resources (page 91)

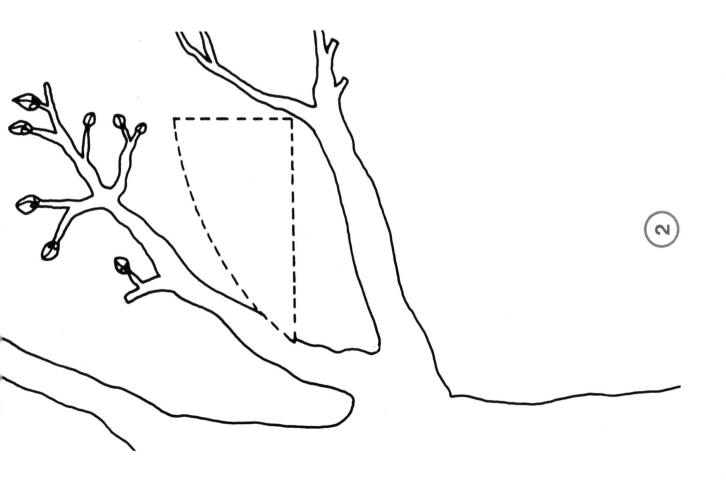

②

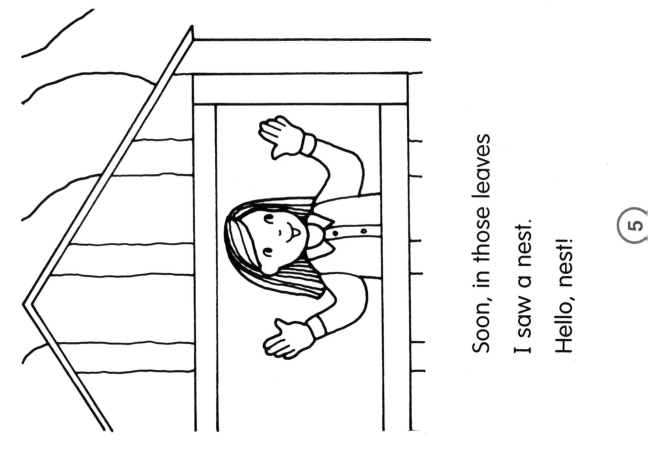

Soon, in those leaves
I saw a nest.
Hello, nest!

5

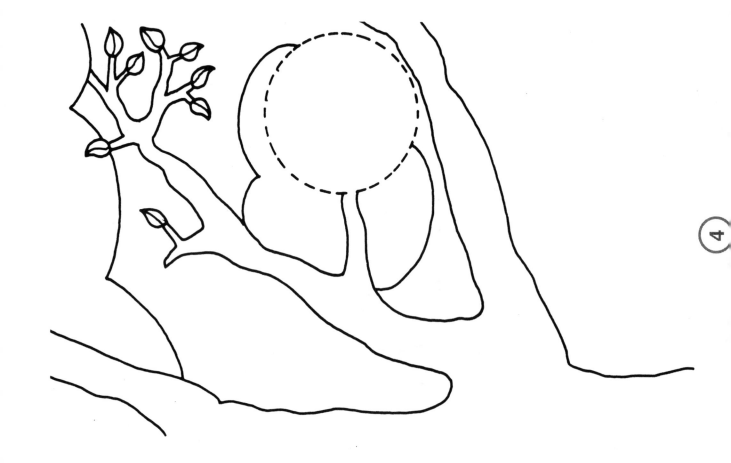

4

Then in that nest
I saw two eggs.
Hello, eggs!

7

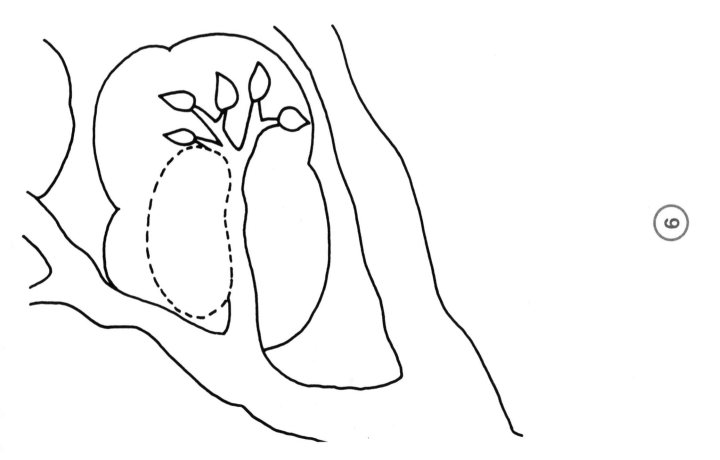

6

And from those eggs

hatched two baby birds.

Hello, birds!

Hello, spring!

Cut & Paste Mini-Books: Around the Year © 2011 by Nancy I. Sanders, Scholastic Teaching Resources (page 94)

(9)

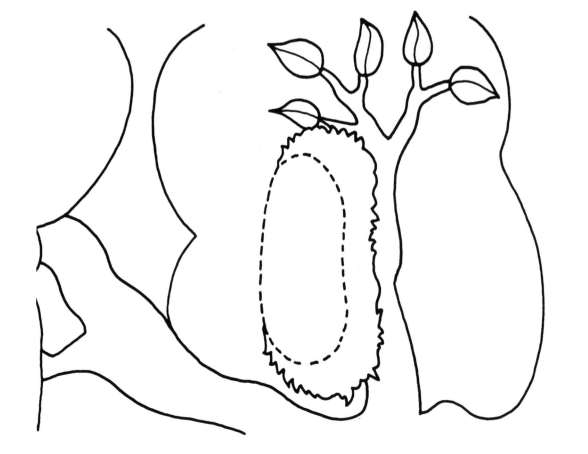

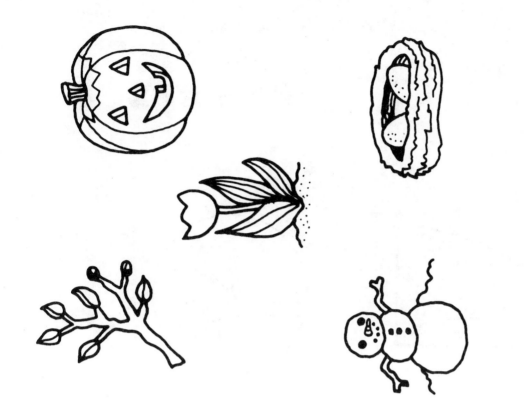

Circle the things you see in spring.

Cut & Paste Mini-Books: Around the Year © 2011 by Nancy I. Sanders, Scholastic Teaching Resources (page 95)

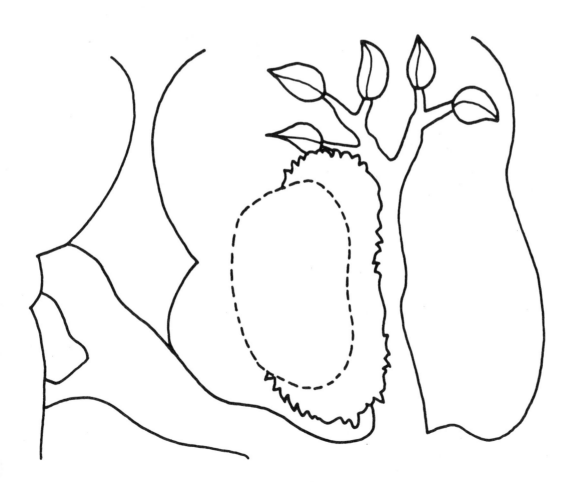

Hello, Spring!

Cut & Paste Patterns

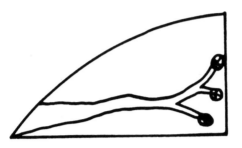

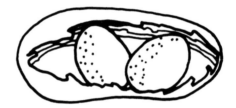

Cut & Paste Mini-Books: Around the Year © 2011 by Nancy I. Sanders, Scholastic Teaching Resources

It's Earth Day!

Getting Started

Explain that Earth Day is a time to celebrate the good things we get from Earth and act on ways to take care of Earth. To help children discover things they can do for Earth Day (and throughout the year), play this game in which they make inferences from picture clues. First, gather pictures of items or activities associated with caring for Earth, such as a recycling container, bicycle, and young tree. Display a picture and say, "It's Earth Day. We can _____ to celebrate." Ask children to think about what the picture might suggest and use that idea to complete the sentence. For example, for the recycling container, they might respond "recycle plastic bottles."

Completing the Mini-Book

Ask children to write their name on the cover, then cut out and glue the patterns onto the pages, as shown. Finally, have them complete the activity on the last page.

Reproducible Pages
mini-book: pages 98–103
patterns: page 104

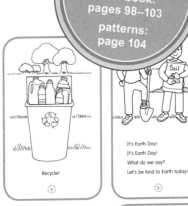

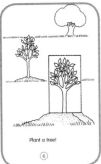

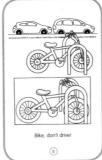

Trace the letters. Read the words.

Taking It Further

Invite children to play Recycle Toss. First, place recyclable plastic, paper, and foam in a pile at one end of the room. Then label each of three large plastic bins with "Paper," "Plastic," or "Foam," and set them a few feet away from the pile. To play, have children take turns choosing an item from the pile and tossing it into the appropriate bin. When finished, remind children that items used in the game can be recycled or reused in some way.

It's Earth Day!

It's Earth Day!

What do we say?

Let's be kind to Earth today!

It's Earth Day!

How Can We Take Care of Earth?

1.

2.

3.

4.

Earth Day Projects

by _____

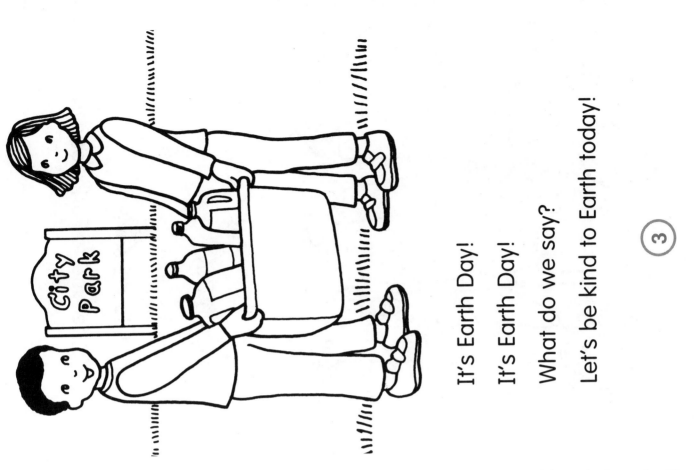

It's Earth Day!

It's Earth Day!

What do we say?

Let's be kind to Earth today!

③

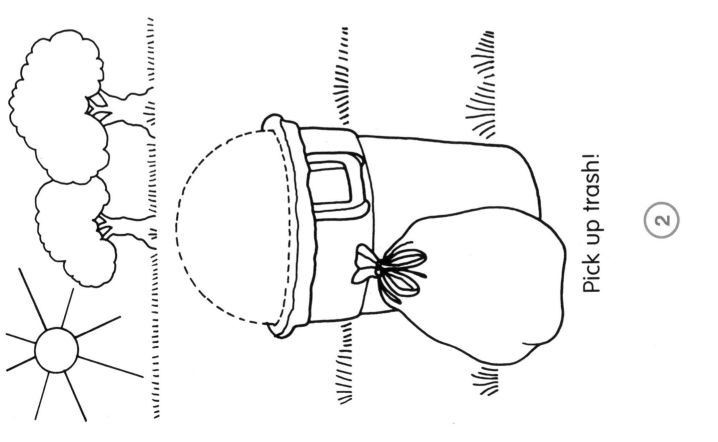

Pick up trash!

②

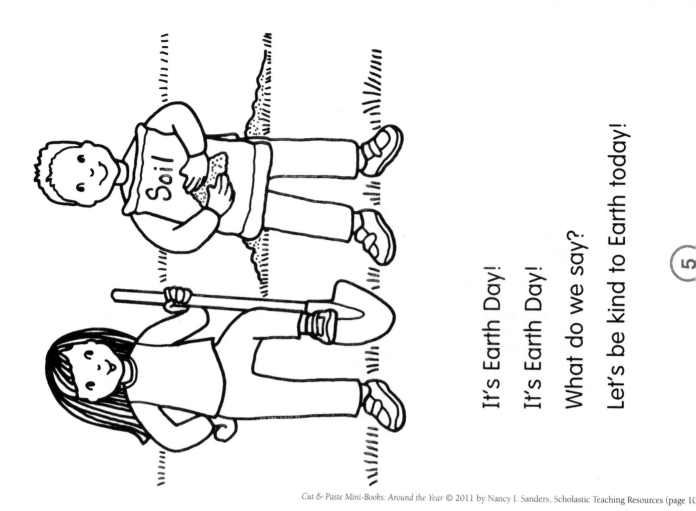

It's Earth Day!

It's Earth Day!

What do we say?

Let's be kind to Earth today!

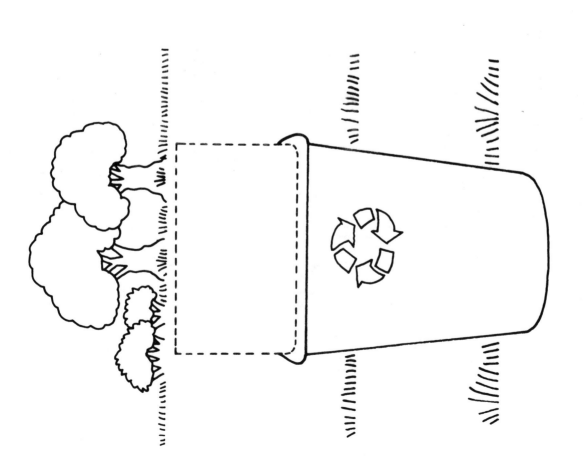

Recycle!

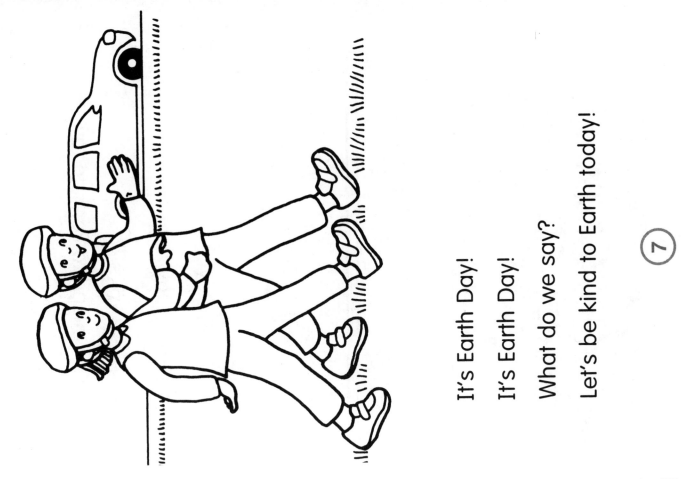

It's Earth Day!

It's Earth Day!

What do we say?

Let's be kind to Earth today!

7

Cut & Paste Mini-Books: Around the Year © 2011 by Nancy I. Sanders, Scholastic Teaching Resources (page 101)

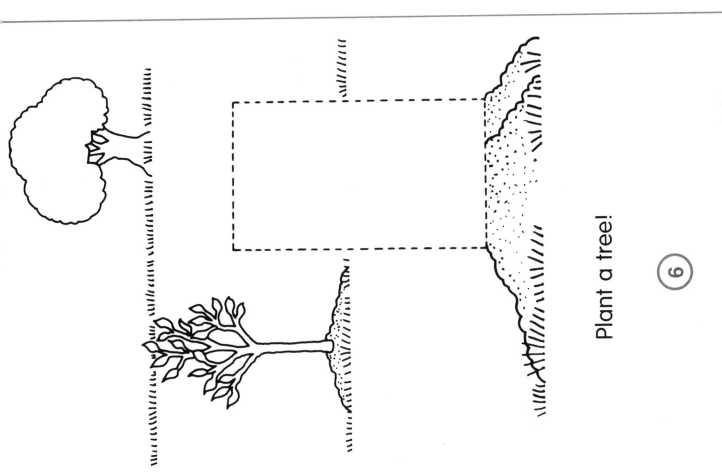

Plant a tree!

6

It's Earth Day!

It's Earth Day!

What do we say?

Let's be kind to Earth today!

Bike, don't drive!

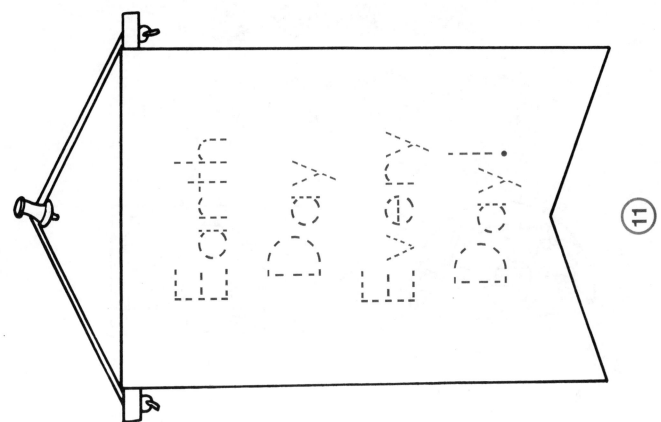

EARTH
DAY
EVERY
DAY!

11

Cut & Paste Mini-Books: Around the Year © 2011 by Nancy I. Sanders, Scholastic Teaching Resources (page 103)

How Can We Take Care of Earth?

1. Pick up trash!

2. Recycle!

3. Plant a tree!

4. Bike, don't drive!

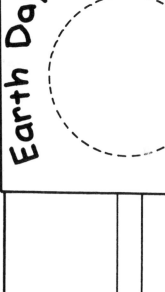

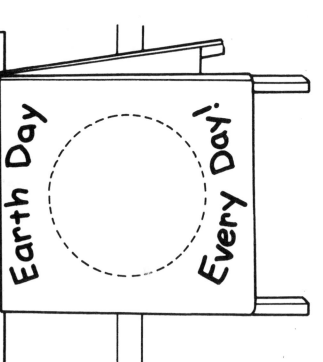

Earth Day

Every Day!

Let's take care of Earth every day!

10

It's Earth Day!

Cut & Paste Patterns

Cut & Paste Mini-Books: Around the Year © 2011 by Nancy I. Sanders, Scholastic Teaching Resources

If You Meet a Gull at the Beach

Getting Started

Ask children to tell about things they can do to stay safe in the sun, such as putting on sunscreen, wearing a hat and sunglasses, staying in the shade, and drinking plenty of water. Then invite children to share about their own experiences in practicing sun safety. For instance, they might describe their sunglasses or hat, tell what kind of shade they prefer sitting in (such as under a tree or in a picnic shelter), or share whether they enjoy drinking plain or flavored water.

Completing the Mini-Book

Ask children to write their name on the cover, then cut out and glue the patterns onto the pages, as shown. Finally, have them complete the activity on the last page.

Reproducible Pages
mini-book: pages 106–111
patterns: page 112

Match each picture to its name.

Taking It Further

Bury a variety of objects in a sand table, including a seashell, flip-flop, plastic shovel, toy crab, and other small beach-related items. Also, hide a few sun safety items such as an empty tube of sunscreen, sunglasses, and a sun visor. Then invite children to take turns digging in the sand until they find an item. When they find one, have them recite this personalized sentence frame similar to the text in the mini-book: *If I meet a gull at the beach, he'll want me to ….* Have them complete the sentence by telling what the gull would want them to do with the item they found. Ask children to bury their item in the sand again at the end of their turn.

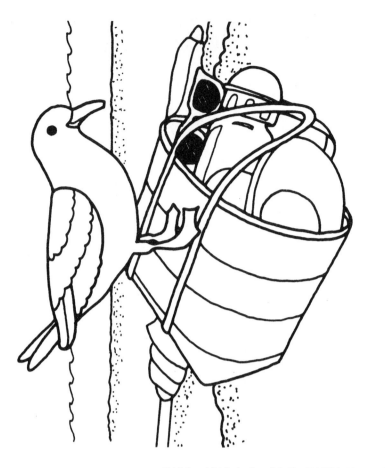

If you meet a gull at the beach,
he'll want you to put on sunscreen.

①

Cut & Paste Mini-Books: Around the Year © 2011 by Nancy I. Sanders, Scholastic Teaching Resources (page 106

If You Meet a Gull at the Beach

by _____

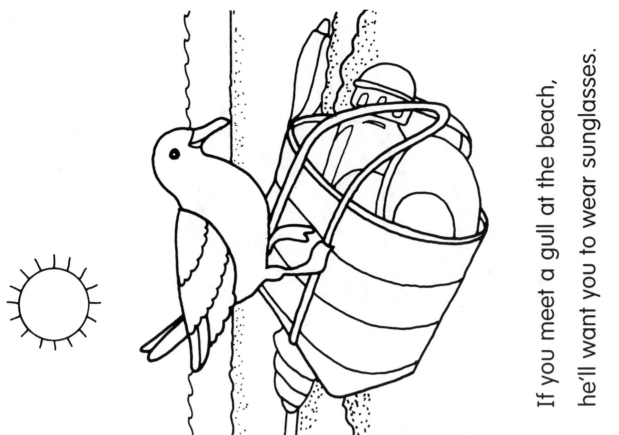

If you meet a gull at the beach,
he'll want you to wear sunglasses.

(3)

Cut & Paste Mini-Books: Around the Year © 2011 by Nancy I. Sanders, Scholastic Teaching Resources (page 107)

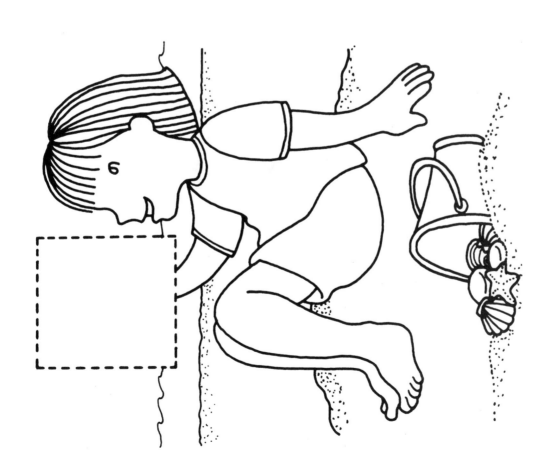

(2)

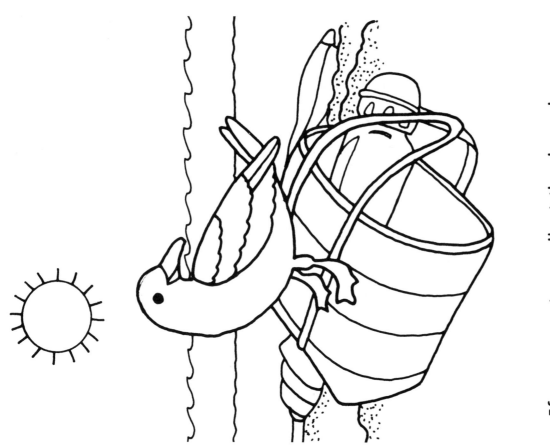

If you meet a gull at the beach,
he'll want you to wear a hat.

⑤

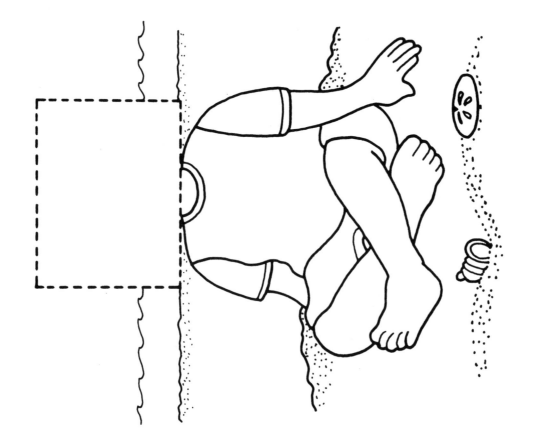

④

If you meet a gull at the beach,
he'll want you to sit in the shade.

⑦

Cut & Paste Mini-Books: Around the Year © 2011 by Nancy I. Sanders, Scholastic Teaching Resources (page 109)

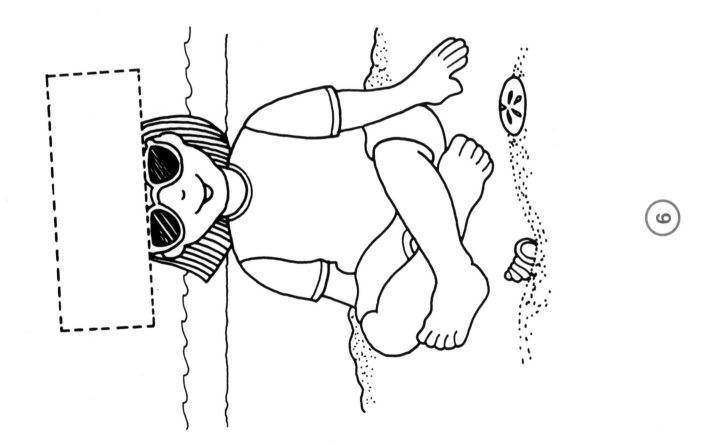

⑥

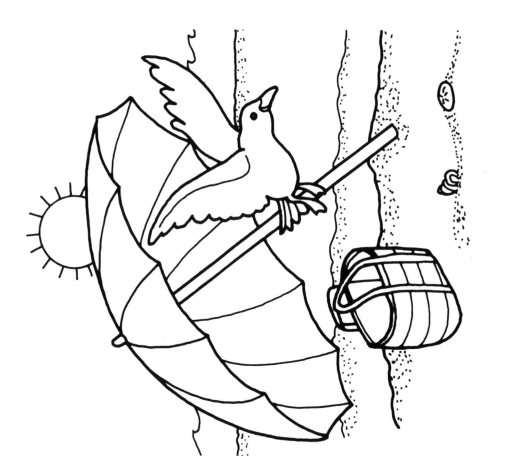

If you meet a gull at the beach,

he'll want you to drink plenty of water.

Have a safe and sunny day!

Cut & Paste Mini-Books: Around the Year © 2011 by Nancy I. Sanders, Scholastic Teaching Resources (page 110

9

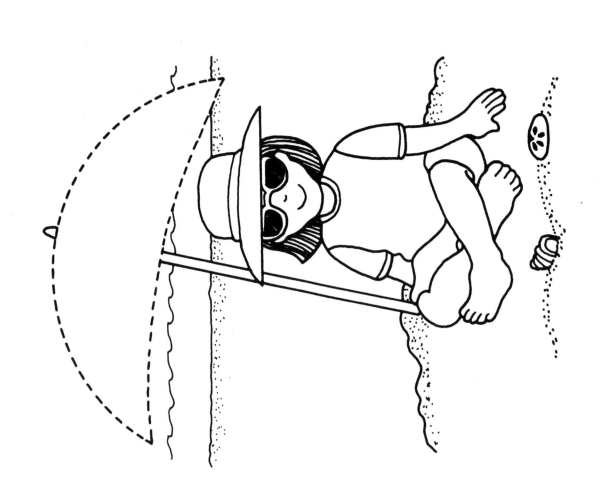

8

sunglasses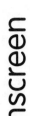

sunscreen

water

hat

Match each picture to its name.

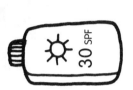

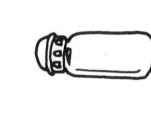

(11)

Cut & Paste Mini-Books: Around the Year © 2011 by Nancy I. Sanders, Scholastic Teaching Resources (page 111)

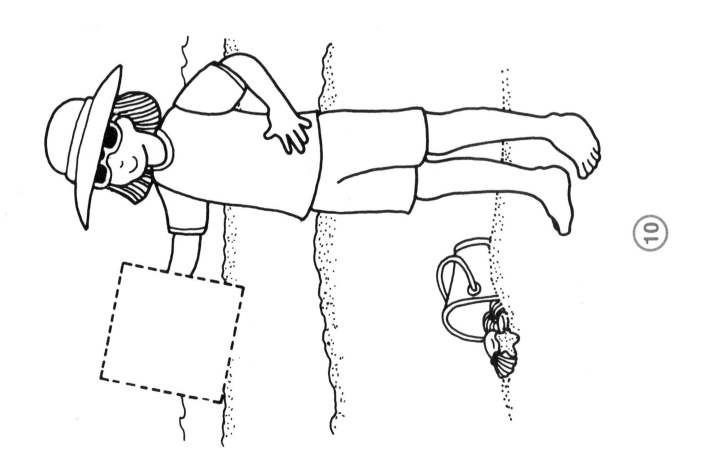

(10)

If You Meet a Gull at the Beach

Cut & Paste Patterns

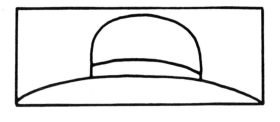

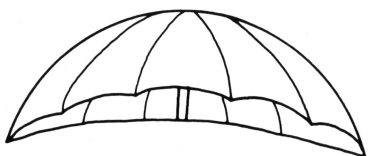

Cut & Paste Mini-Books: Around the Year © 2011 by Nancy I. Sanders, Scholastic Teaching Resources

The Fourth of July

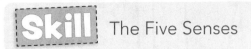

Skill The Five Senses

Getting Started

Divide a display into five sections and title it "Celebrate the Five Senses!" Label each of five large index cards with one of the following: *see, hear, smell, taste,* or *touch.* Then display one word card at a time and use that word to complete this question: *What things can I ___ to celebrate?* Ask children to name items related to the Fourth of July to answer the question. List their responses in a section on the display, then attach the corresponding word card to that section. Later, invite children to draw items from each list to add to the display.

Completing the Mini-Book

Ask children to write their name on the cover, then cut out and glue the patterns onto the pages, as shown. Finally, have them complete the activity on the last page.

Reproducible Pages
mini-book: pages 114–119
patterns: page 120

The Fourth of July
by _____

I **smell** sweet corn and apple pie.
①

②

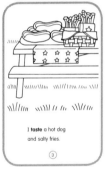
I **taste** a hot dog and salty fries.
③

④

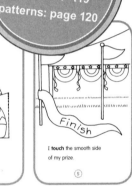
I **touch** the smooth side of my prize.
⑤

⑥

I **see** the flag I hold up high.
⑦

⑧

I **hear** loud fireworks in the sky. Happy Fourth of July!
⑨

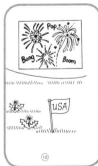
⑩

Draw fireworks in the sky. Color them red, white, and blue.
⑪

Draw fireworks, then color them red, white, and blue.

Taking It Further

Invite children to imagine they are at a Fourth of July celebration, complete with picnic and fireworks. Have them fill in this sentence frame by naming things they might experience during the event: "At the celebration, I tasted a..." (*hot dog,* for example). After children share, change the sentence by replacing the verb (*tasted*) with *saw, smelled, heard,* or *felt.* Once children have filled in a sentence for each of the verbs, invite them to write about and illustrate each imagined sensory experience on a separate sheet of paper. Finally, help them bind their pages into a book.

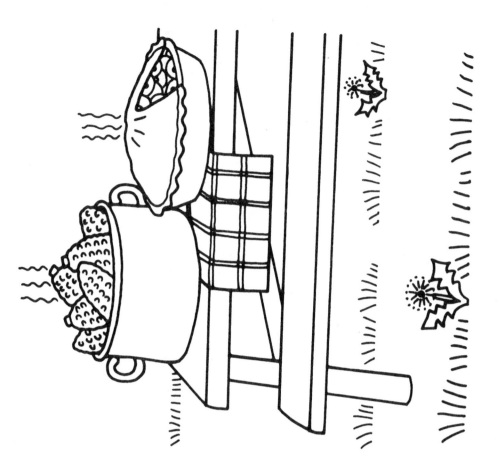

I **smell** sweet corn
and apple pie.

Cut & Paste Mini-Books: Around the Year © 2011 by Nancy I. Sanders, Scholastic Teaching Resources (page 114

The Fourth of July

by _____

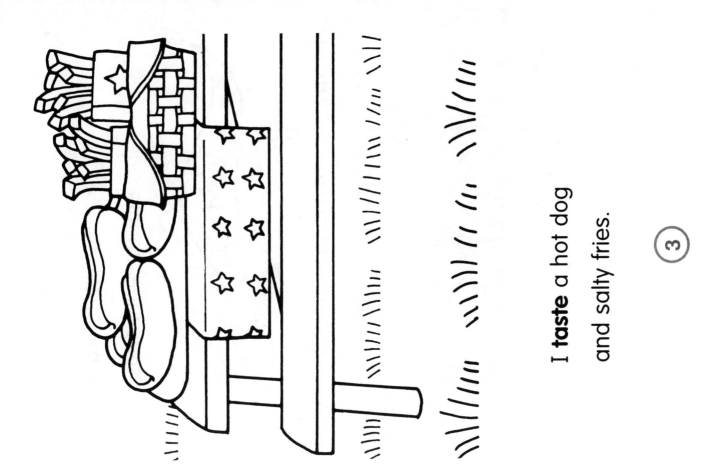

I **taste** a hot dog
and salty fries.

③

②

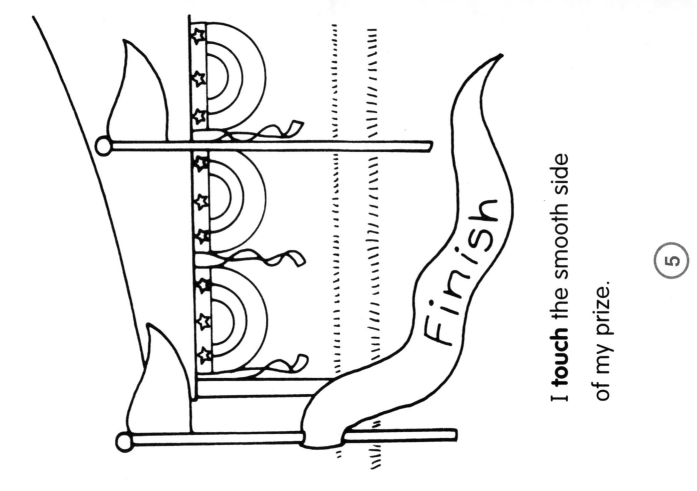

I touch the smooth side
of my prize.

⑤

④

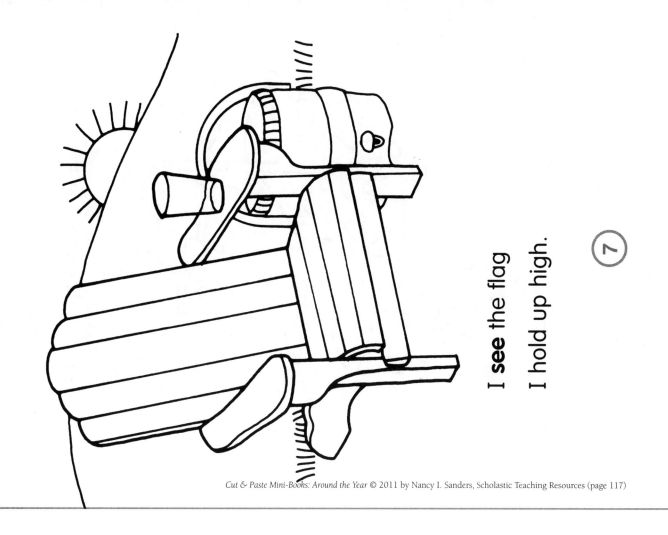

I see the flag

I hold up high.

⑦

⑥

I **hear** loud fireworks in the sky.

Happy Fourth of July!

Cut & Paste Mini-Books: Around the Year © 2011 by Nancy I. Sanders, Scholastic Teaching Resources (page 118

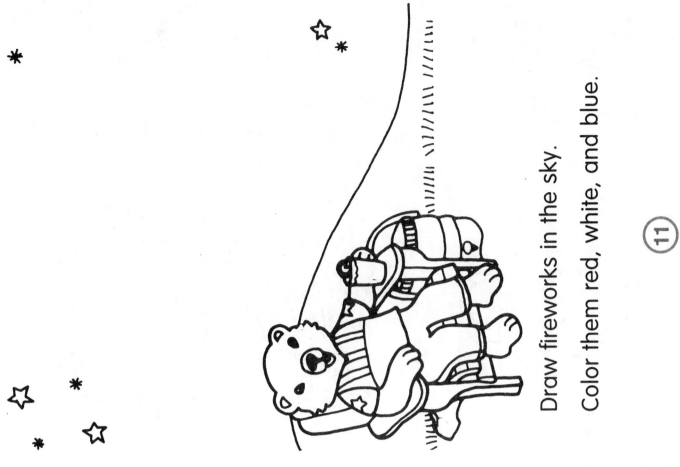

Draw fireworks in the sky.
Color them red, white, and blue.

(11)

Cut & Paste Mini-Books: Around the Year © 2011 by Nancy I. Sanders, Scholastic Teaching Resources (page 119)

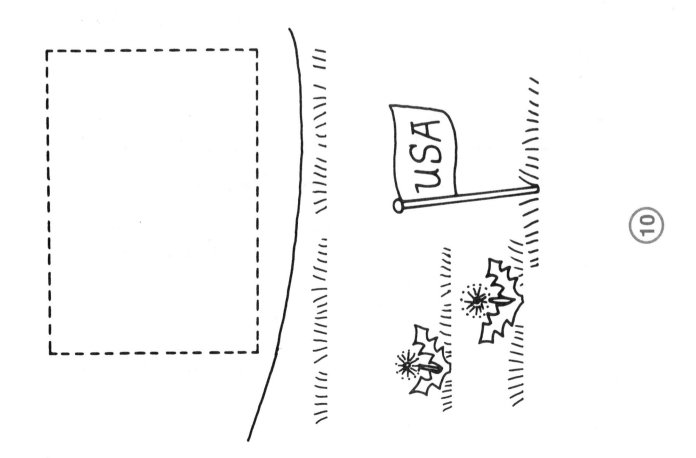

USA

(10)

The Fourth of July

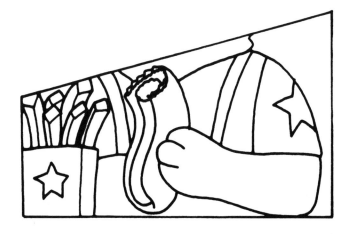

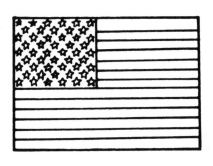

Cut & Paste Mini-Books: Around the Year © 2011 by Nancy I. Sanders, Scholastic Teaching Resources

Candles on the Cake

Skill Counting

Getting Started

List children's names on chart paper. Read the names aloud, one at a time, asking children to tell how old they are when they hear their name. Write the number for their age by their name, then invite children to draw that many candles by the number. After every child has had a turn to draw candles, review the children's names and ages. For each name called, have the class chorally count the candles as you point to each one by that child's name.

Completing the Mini-Book

Ask children to write their name on the cover, then cut out and glue the patterns onto the pages, as shown. Finally, have them complete the activity on the last page.

Reproducible Pages
mini-book:
pages 122–127
patterns: page 128

Candles on the Cake

by _____

Birthdays are super.
Birthdays are great.
Put **1** candle
on the cupcake for Kate.
Happy Birthday, Kate!

①

②

Birthdays are super.
Birthdays are sweet.
Put **2** candles
on the cake for Pete.
Happy Birthday, Pete!

③

④

Birthdays are super.
Birthdays are swell.
Put **3** candles
on the cake for Nell.
Happy Birthday, Nell!

⑤

⑥

Birthdays are super.
Birthdays are grand.
Put **4** candles
on the cake for Dan.
Happy Birthday, Dan!

⑦

⑧

Birthdays are fun
whatever you do.
Put enough candles
on the cake for you.

⑨

I am _____ years old!

⑩

Carmen is 7 years old today.
Draw 7 candles on her cake.

⑪

Glue on candles equal to the child's age. Write the number.

Draw 7 candles on the cake.

Taking It Further

Give each child a strip of paper to represent a candle. Help children write their name, birthday month, and age on their candles. If desired, they might also decorate their candle. Then have children mingle with each other, checking their candles to find classmates who have a birthday in the same months. Once they are grouped by months, ask children to count how many are in their group. Record the findings, by month, then compare and discuss the results with children to discover which month has the most or least number of birthdays.

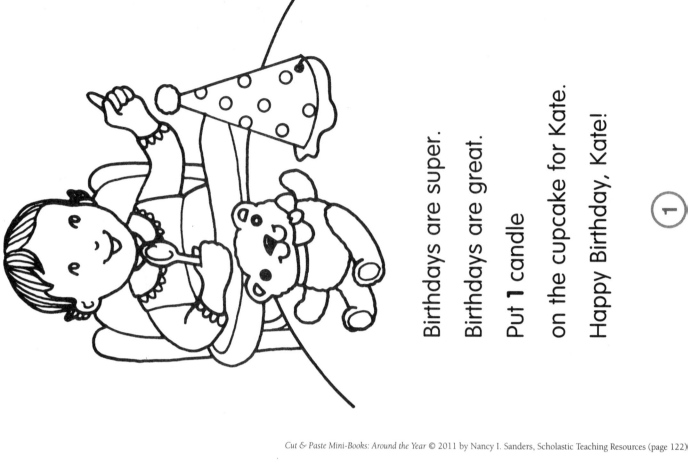

Birthdays are super.

Birthdays are great.

Put **1** candle

on the cupcake for Kate.

Happy Birthday, Kate!

(1)

Cut & Paste Mini-Books: Around the Year © 2011 by Nancy I. Sanders, Scholastic Teaching Resources (page 122)

Candles on the Cake

Happy Birthday

Birthday Candles

by _____

Birthdays are super.

Birthdays are sweet.

Put **2** candles

on the cake for Pete.

Happy Birthday, Pete!

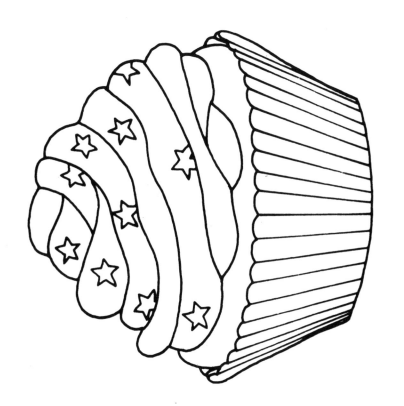

Birthdays are super.

Birthdays are swell.

Put **3** candles

on the cake for Nell.

Happy Birthday, Nell!

Cut & Paste Mini-Books: Around the Year © 2011 by Nancy I. Sanders, Scholastic Teaching Resources (page 12

5

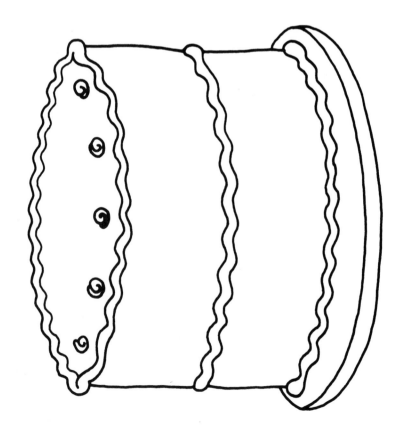

4

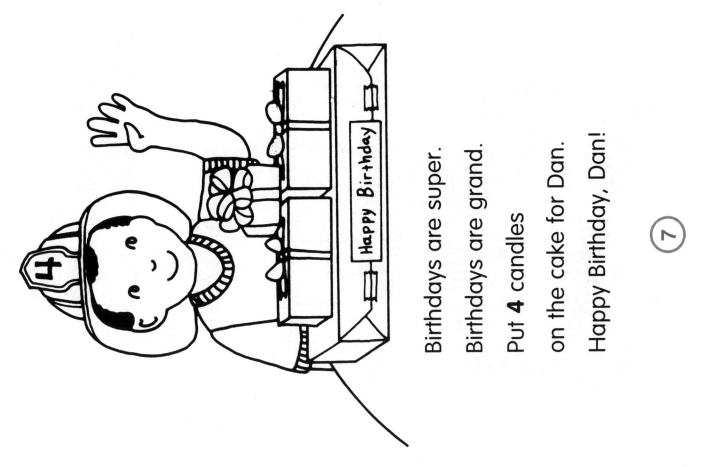

Birthdays are super.

Birthdays are grand.

Put **4** candles

on the cake for Dan.

Happy Birthday, Dan!

Cut & Paste Mini-Books: Around the Year © 2011 by Nancy I. Sanders, Scholastic Teaching Resources (page 125)

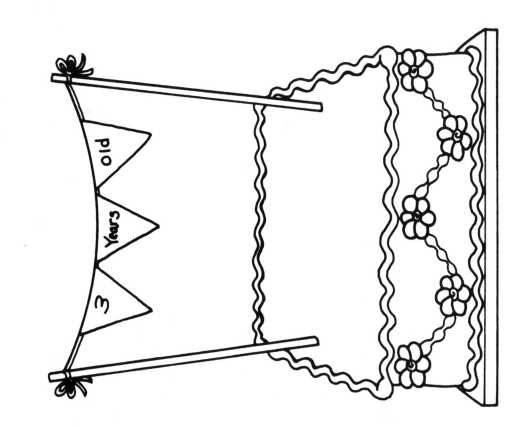

Birthdays are fun
whatever you do.
Put enough candles
on the cake for you.

Cut & Paste Mini-Books: Around the Year © 2011 by Nancy I. Sanders, Scholastic Teaching Resources (page 126)

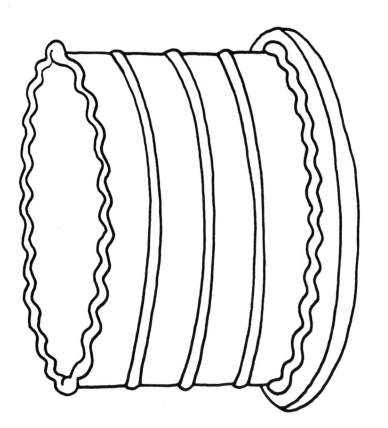

Carmen is 7 years old today.

Draw 7 candles on her cake.

Cut & Paste Mini-Books: Around the Year © 2011 by Nancy I. Sanders, Scholastic Teaching Resources (page 127)

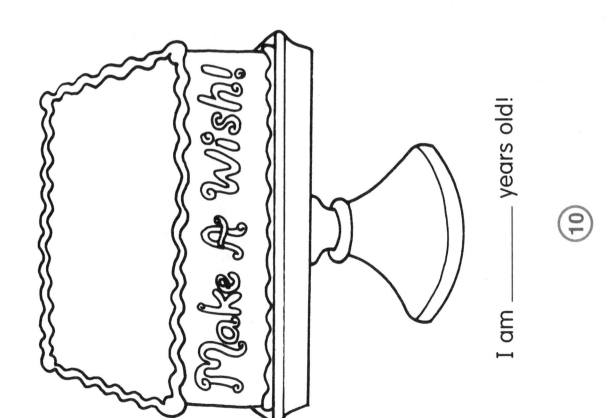

Make it wish!

I am _____ years old!

Candles on the Cake

Cut & Paste Patterns

Cut & Paste Mini-Books: Around the Year © 2011 by Nancy I. Sanders, Scholastic Teaching Resources